You Can Complete That Book

2-29-20

To Davida –
Write On!
Hope to read your
book soon!

You Can Complete That Book

Love,

Leslie Keenan

Leslie Keenan

Published by:

The Printed Voice
PO Box 1071
Novato, CA 94945

Interior Design and Layout by: Margaux Joy DeNador
Edited by: Katherine Dieter

ISBN: 978-0-9840557-7-7

First Printing, October, 2016
Printed in the USA on acid-free paper
10 9 8 7 6 5 4 3 2 1

To all my writing students
Your dedication and courage inspire me every day

Acknowledgements

I have many people to thank for helping me along the way. First I must thank all the "aunties" who volunteered to babysit for me so that I could continue writing after my daughter was born: Katherine Dieter, Maureen Smith, Laura Deutsch, Vivian Bobka, Christy Michaels. It really does take a village.

Katherine Dieter is an editor par excellence and she has done her usual stellar job here. My writing students listened patiently and kept encouraging me to finish so they could stop taking notes and have their own personal copy. And many of them graciously contributed their stories and their exercises for me to share. My sister, Jenny Keenan Smith carefully read the final page proofs with her usual insight, catching a few gaffs and improving the writing.

I am grateful to Margaux Joy DeNador for the interior design of this book. She captured its spirit in a way that surprised and delighted me. I felt I was in capable hands the whole way.

Table of Contents 

Introduction

I love writers. I love hanging out with writers. I love that my job allows me to work with writers every day. I love getting down in the dirt with a writer who is grappling with some difficult issue about how to fit a new idea into the existing book, or who can't seem to let go of parts that don't fit anymore. I love being on the other end of the phone when a writer just needs some reassurance that this really will be a book one day. I love how writers love words and can get satisfaction out of finding the precise word that fits what they are trying to say. I love how writers appreciate a well-written book. I love the way writers think. And I even love how writers always, always, always disparage their own writing, or deny that they are in fact writers.

I have been working with writers in one form or another for thirty years. Somewhat by instinct at first, and later through lots of experience, I learned how the creative process works. I know the stages one most go through in any creative endeavor, and how a writer goes through those stages. I was labeled a muse early on by one of my authors and realized that's what I do. I think of myself as a midwife to the creative process. I know where you will need to push and where you will need to just breathe for a bit. I have written this book to distill what I know works in easing a writer through the difficulties in writing, to actually complete that book.

I usually teach the ideas found here in classes that are from four to six weeks long. The format I use includes homework assignments and commitments each week. I have designed this book so that you can approach it that way, and read a chapter a week and do the assignments. Or, you can turn directly to the chapter where you are stuck and needing help. Since commitment and good habits are two very crucial pieces to the writing process, I encourage you to be willing to write down at the very least when you are going to write and for how long each week, and check in weekly on your progress. One thing I know that helps with completion is creating small milestones and achieving them. You may want to get a separate small notebook where you keep track; or, if you are industrious and techno-savvy, you may want to create a spreadsheet to keep track. The important thing is to see that you are showing up and making progress even when you feel you aren't or it's slower going than you'd like.

I hope this book will help you feel that you are not alone, and that in fact you are part of a wonderful community of writers. (The beauty of the written word is that you are even part of the history of writers who have long since moved on, many leaving wonderful tips in one form or another on their own writing process.) If you ever find that you want a more tangible kind of support, I also include suggestions in the appendix on how to form a writer's group. Some writers I have worked with enjoy having an accountability partner. This is a fellow writer to whom you make commitments and then either just keep track for each other, or actually read each others' writing as you progress. Some people do this remotely via email and telephone; some simply meet at a coffee shop and sit at the same table to write for an hour with company. (This only works if you don't spend the entire time talking to each other!) Put these ideas to work in your own writing practice and you can complete that book.

Chapter 1

Where Are You Stuck?

If you are reading this book, you have probably already started writing what you hope will be a book. Congratulations! You have already gotten through a hard part. I always say that starting and finishing are the two most difficult things in writing. Fear of starting is fear of failure. (If I never put anything down, I can always imagine that when I do it will be perfect.) Fear of finishing is fear of success—and, in my experience, this is where more people get stuck. It's like that famous Marianne Williamson quote (often mistakenly attributed to Nelson Mandela, who quoted it in his 1994 Inauguration speech):

"Our deepest fear is not that we are inadequate. Our deepest fear is that we are powerful beyond measure. It is our light, not our darkness that most frightens us. We ask ourselves, Who am I to be brilliant, gorgeous, talented, fabulous? Actually, who are you *not* to be? You are a child of God. Your playing small does not serve the world."

I've put this book together to help writers like you get past this stuck place and move forward. I promise you that if you are willing and do all the exercises I suggest, you *can* finish.

I've been working with writers for my whole career, first as a traditional editor in mainstream publishing houses, then as a literary agent, and then as a writing coach and teacher. But all this time, I've been doing the same thing: helping writers recognize the books they have in them, and helping them get those books out into form and into the world. To date, I've worked on more than 100 published books. I know what it takes to move from a vague idea, or some notes jotted on a page, to a complete book. I know where it's going to get hard, where you need to keep breathing, and most of all, that there is an end.

I'm going to help you figure out where you are exactly, and where in the book you can find what you need to do to get moving again.

Here are some possibilities:

* You just got your toes wet and then stopped (maybe you got overwhelmed, maybe you had "no time"). Start with the following section on the Inner Critic.
* You finished 100 pages and everything was going fine; then, you lost momentum. This could be fear of success or failure, in which case, start with the following section on the Inner Critic. It may be a structural issue. Go to the structural material in Chapter 4, "Structure."
* You finished your first draft, but don't know what to do now. Go to Chapter 5, "Editing Your First Draft."
* You are moving through the book; you are not really "stuck," you just need a pep talk. Read all the way through.
* You want to write, but don't have time. See Chapter 3, "Keep Going"
* You always wanted to write, you have fragments sitting in drawers, but you "lack discipline" or never finish; you have "too many ideas." You have mastered the art of flow and need to work on refinement. Check out Chapter 3, "Keep Going"

and Chapter 4, "Structure"—especially the section called "Flow vs. Structure."

* You always wanted to write, you know you have a story to tell, but you don't know how to begin. Start here:

Many people who come into my class think there's some simple thing they can do (be more disciplined, try some new writing gimmick) that will get them to finish their book. What most people don't realize is the scope of the task at hand. Writers are the most courageous people I know. To show up every day to a blank screen or page, to be willing to fight off the demons shouting in your head, to ignore every fear you've ever had and begin putting words on that page, and then courageously continue without scratching them out; well, I am always astounded. Because what I know that you might not know yet is that there are lots of things going on under the surface that need to be sorted out if you want to get to that happy place of writing easily and smoothly in flow, and finishing the manuscript.

In this book I'm going to take you, gently, through the stages I know you must go through in the creative process. I'm going to hold your hand, and coach you. And if you stick with it and are willing, I know things will shift.

What is a writer? When they first come to my class, many students can't or won't even call themselves writers. They think writers are people who have been published already, or who make their living by writing, or who have gotten positive reviews in the *New York Times*. Or, maybe a writer for you is someone who devotes him- or herself to writing but is always struggling, living in poverty, and devoted to and making sacrifices for their "art." Anything less is not worthy of the title "writer."

Let me tell you my definition of a writer. A writer is someone who writes. That's it. A writer is not someone who talks about writing, or thinks about writing, or imagines what he or she will do once the book is written and they are on *Oprah*, or imagines casting the movie before writing a word. A writer is someone who writes. Once you begin this process, and commit to it, you begin to realize that that is plenty. There is a lot of work, energy and effort required to show up and write, and to keep doing so. When I first began teaching my classes, they were held in a bookstore, in a room filled with books. I'd always point to those books and say, what is the difference between the people who wrote those books and you? The answer is, they kept writing. They kept writing through all the difficulties and hardships, and they kept writing after they got book deals and contracts, and they kept writing after that. It's the writing itself that matters, not all the trappings.

Our culture doesn't really encourage creativity. From a very early age, instead of learning about the all-embracing, free-flowing, creative energy available to us, we have been learning about judgment and, often, criticism. I can remember in kindergarten having to draw within the lines, and feeling much shame and embarrassment for not being able to do it. How much more did we learn to criticize writing! There were so many rules. You had to spell correctly, you had to use good grammar, and you had to stick to the topic. And worse, your teacher corrected your mistakes in red pen for all to see. (When I edit, I always use a blue pen because we have such harsh associations with red ink.)

Before thinking about this too much, I want you to do this exercise. Set a timer and write for five minutes nonstop, and no more. We are looking to get to those unconscious voices we carry around in our heads all the time and aren't even aware of. Just let it rip. Keep your pen on the page and just get it out. Ready? Okay. I want you to write out all the reasons you can't write, or why you can't write this book in particular:

Reasons I can't write:

1.
2.
3.
4.
5.
6.
7.
8.
9.
10.

Are you done? Pretty surprising isn't it? Almost invariably, when I have people read their responses in class, there is one person who can't write because they can't spell, and one who can't write because they don't know grammar. Thinking "I'm too old," or "I'm not disciplined" are also common. But usually there are some deeper, more vicious responses, like: I'm not good enough, I don't know what I'm talking about, I'm not qualified, others have written similar books, better. There's nothing new, it's been done before. It's a corny idea. It will be boring. Who do I think I am? Some may be what I think of as "legitimate" reasons, like "I don't have time" or "I'm afraid I don't know how." The purpose of this exercise is to get to hear and know the voice of the Inner Critic. You may have heard this term before. The Inner Critic is the voice inside us that developed at a very early age, usually by about two years old. It had a very legitimate purpose:

to prevent us from being criticized in the outside world. The trouble is, in order to prevent outside criticism, your inner critic has to be more severe than the most severe critic of your outer world. So if, for instance, you had a particularly harsh teacher, your critic had to be even stricter to make sure the teacher wouldn't criticize you. And, as I said, our culture in general is quite harsh. I have found it to be true that most of the writers I work with have a very harsh inner critic. I don't know why, I just know it is so. Do you start to see why sitting down to write can be such a difficult process? When you have this harsh inner critic hovering over your shoulder, how can you possibly say anything that will be good enough? This is why many people can't even get one word onto the page.

Look back over your list. Can you identify the voice of your critic? Are some of your reasons legitimate? Can you sort through to pinpoint the harshness and unreasonableness of the critic? One sure way to recognize it is that it makes you not want to write at all. You might think, "What's the use?" or you might think "Who do I think I am that I can write this?" or that people will care? Take note of the reasons that make you feel this way. It is revealing to you who your critic is. If you are having trouble identifying it, you may want to take a minute and do the exercise again now that you know its purpose.

Now, let's take it a step further. You probably won't like this exercise as much, but do it anyway. This one exercise can make the biggest difference in your ability to write. I want you to draw a picture of your inner critic. If you are having trouble, try using your non-dominant hand. It doesn't have to be a good or an accurate drawing. It can be a symbol or colors and shapes that don't look like anything real. It could be a stick figure with a balloon showing the words the critic says. I just want it to be expressive. Set the timer again for three minutes. Ready? Go.

Are you finished? Good. Now, I want you to tear the picture out of the book and take a moment to walk the picture to the other side of the room and place it on the floor or a chair. Then, come back here.

Okay, you may, in your conscious mind, have thought that was silly. To your subconscious mind, however, this step is enormous. What you are saying to your creative self is, I'm creating a safe environment for you to come out and play. I'm going to protect you from the voice of the Inner Critic when you are at your most vulnerable and fragile. I'm going to let you create something before we begin to decide what it is.

When you bake bread, you don't expect to eat it when it's dough sitting in a bowl with a towel over it. The yeast is working, and expanding the dough; and then, it needs to be punched down and kneaded, and it needs to sit some more. Then, it needs to go in the oven and bake for a specified length of time. Only *then* can you take it out and slice it and see how it tastes.

The point is not to get mad at the critic and try to cut that voice out entirely. If you try to ignore the critic, get rid of it, say it's bad, you are actually giving it more power. (This is just a psychological truth.) What I'd like you to do (and what these exercises have already begun doing for you) is to *recognize* this voice, and see that *it's not necessarily the truth.* Then, I want you to begin to listen more often to the other voices inside you, and begin to give the positive, encouraging ones a little more credence.

What is actually more effective at diminishing the harshness of the critic, is acknowledging it, and honoring it for what it is trying to do. The critic's *only* concern and *only* job, is to protect you. The trouble is, it thinks the only way to do that properly is to never let you write a word. The creative self is vulnerable to the critic and won't come out if it is present.

Instead of trying to eliminate the critic, try saying this: I acknowledge you, I honor you, thank you for the service you've given me over the years. Right now, however, I'm in the creative flow, and your input is not needed until later. You have laser-sharp observation skills, that put to use too soon, will prevent us from having any bread at all. What you are saying to your creative self is, go ahead. Play with things. Squish the dough up and punch it some more. Write badly. Write anything you want. I'm giving you time here to expand.

If you address the critic's fears, and assure it that you are not jumping blindly into the lion's den, the critic is far more likely to lessen its death grip on your soul. Instead, set up careful checkpoints such as friendly readers to review early drafts, professional editors to review later drafts, and a proofreader to review the final draft to help ensure that you are not attacked or criticized. If you acknowledge the critic and honor it while at the same time giving it boundaries, you are taking the debilitating edge off of it. It's Darth Vader with his mask off. In writing we do need a critical function in order to edit. The thing is, we want that input at the right time and in the right way. Not when it's dough we're working with, but when it's bread.

I have often made agreements with clients' inner critics. Your inner critic may be saying: but if I don't do this, she/he won't get anything done. She/he's lazy and irresponsible and just wants to goof off instead of sticking to the schedule. What I do is suggest to the Inner Critic that we give this other method a try before making those decisions (judgments). We'll look at some evidence. I'll say, "Let's give my client six months free to write whatever without any comment from you. Then, on that specific date, we will invite you back in and hear your opinion on the client's progress, and we can make a new agreement about how to proceed from there."

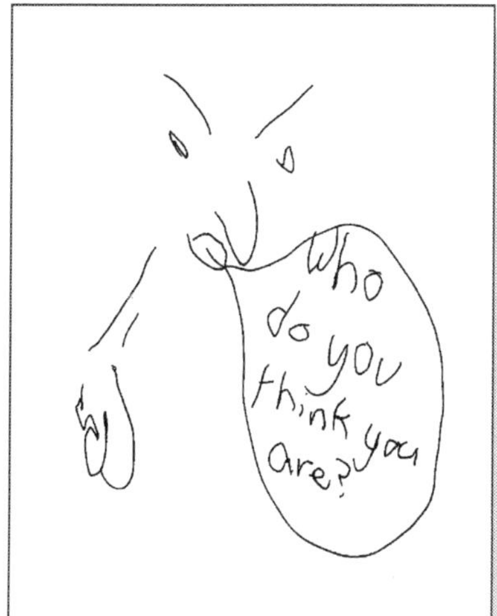
Who do you think you are?

NO

What makes you think you can write?

My Inner Critic
It is Dangerous To put things in Writing! Forget about Writing and Forget About Singing!

A sample Inner Critic Contract:

I, ______________________________, commit to writing in flow for ______ months.

My inner critic agrees to sit on the sidelines until this process is complete.

On __________________________ (specific date) I agree to let my critic look over the material, and I will take note of the critic's opinion at that time.

Signed: ______________________________

(your name)

Agreed: ______________________________

(your inner critic)

You may want to keep your drawing and use it as a physical reminder to put your critic outside the door when you write. Or, you may choose to burn it (which is what I often offer to do for my students).

A Critic-Free Zone

Why is it so important to have a critic-free zone? Because that's what you need in order to create. We need to write badly in order to be able to write well. And the critic won't let us write badly. So, invite your critic to wait outside the door while you are writing. Or better yet, give it some interesting problem to work on in the corner.

Now, before we move on, there's one more exercise we have to do. I think of it as the antidote to the critic exercises. This is another five minute writing exercise. Ready? Okay. I want you to write down all the reasons you *have* to write this book.

Reasons I have to write:

1.

2.

3.

4.

5.

6.

7.

8.

9.

10.

I love doing this exercise after we do the critic exercise in class. As people read their reasons for writing, the energy in the room changes completely. I always notice that while the reasons *not* to write seem flimsy and untrue, the reasons *to* write seem to come from deep within, they seem to have strength behind them, and they are valid. Each of these lists is always very personal and yet universal. I include one from Blanca Florido (with her kind permission):

Reasons why I had to write this book:

1. *There is, apparently, a Faerie standing over my shoulder dictating it. It's the only explanation for how this is pouring into me.*

2. *I do not seem to be able to stop it. The pictures flow in like water, and if I don't write them down, my mind might explode.*

3. *Because it's there.*

4. *If I don't, the story won't be told, at least not by me, in the way that I'm hearing and seeing it. And it has to be told.*

5. *Because I just can't not write it. It pesters me constantly unless I'm paying attention to it.*

6. *If I am not writing, there is a dark, empty place inside of me.*

7. *There are things to be said that people have to hear.*

8. *Because I have to. Like my protagonist, the story came to me whether I wanted it or not, and continues to insist that I step into who I am by writing it.*

9. *Because when I'm not writing it, I get very cranky.*

10. *Because when I'm writing it, my heart sings with joy.*

I often will tell people they may want to post this list by their writing space, to remind them why they are doing it.

The writing process requires two separate and distinct functions, each one important. We might consider them to be the right and left brain functions—the right brain being the flow, the left brain being the structure. This is probably true in all creative processes; if you are a painter, however it's a lot more obvious when you are in one and then the other. In writing, you need to have the flow come, and you need to edit what you write. The thing is, you can't do both at the same time. Many people find themselves stuck, with "writers' block," because they are trying to do both at once. I always imagine it as if you are typing on an old manual typewriter and two keys cross each other and get stuck. I think of the right brain function, the flow, as a flowing stream of running water. The editing function acts to turn the valve off, cutting down the flow. It might work something like this. You write a sentence, and even as the words are coming out, you think, "No, I should start it differently," or "That's not precisely what I'm trying to say," so you go back and work on that sentence until you feel it's *perfect*. Meanwhile, you've forgotten what the next sentence is. When you are writing in flow, it just comes pouring out of you, easily. If you can let that flow happen, ride it to the very end, and *then* go back and edit it; you won't be cutting off the flow. It can take discipline to keep moving forward, ignoring every little mistake as you write. I recommend just moving forward, and not even worrying about typos or spelling mistakes (as long as you can decipher what you wrote!). Rather than stop my flow, I will often type a bracketed note to myself like this: [add more specifics on fears here] so that when I go back I know what to add, but I don't let it stop me. If you are writing nonfiction or fiction that requires research, you might let yourself write ahead, and then go look things up to make sure your facts are correct.

So, when do you let yourself go back and edit? This will be different for each person. I always say that the proof is in the pudding. You know you've found your balance of flow and editing when the flow keeps coming. If your flow stops, then you need to back off on your editing. For some people, it can take writing the whole first draft out and letting it sit for a while, before going back and editing. Other people may be able to write something in the morning and edit it that afternoon. Very rarely, there are people who seem to be able to edit a little bit as they go along—but it's usually making minor corrections.

One of my students had a morning routine that worked well for her. She'd come out to the kitchen to have her coffee, read over the pages she'd written the day before, and make tiny corrections. Then she'd move to her office and write in flow. If your writing has been stuck for a long time, I recommend not editing at all for a while.

There's another thing to watch out for. Most writers I know say that while they are writing in flow, they are often thrilled with what they are working on. When I wrote my first book, there were times when I thought, "This is great! This is the best book ever written!" That kind of high from writing is often immediately followed by the backlash. This is usually twenty minutes to a day after you've stopped writing. "What was I thinking? I don't know how to write. This is dreck. It doesn't even make sense!" Please, whatever you do, don't act on these feelings! Especially, don't toss what you've written. These feelings will pass. You are not yet able to judge clearly. This is why so many writers let their material sit for a while before they go back to it. (Stephen King puts the first draft of his novel away for six weeks.) Only when you can look at it in a detached manner and say, "This is good. That is not exactly what I meant to say, I could write it more clearly" is it safe to begin to make those changes. Stephen King's wife rescued his first rough sketch of *Carrie* from the trash saying, "I think there's something here."

Jane Austen seemed to have a useful system to balance flow and editing. When she was writing in her prime (and keep in mind that she revised two old manuscripts and wrote three new ones in approximately seven years) she would work on a new novel in the morning. In the afternoon, she would edit the novel she had already completed. That way, she was always doing both, so she had the enjoyment of flow writing to keep her entertained, and the discipline of editing, but working on material that was no longer fresh, so she had a more detached perspective on it.

You will need to experiment, and see what works best for you.

By the way, if you are writing on the computer, and using the Microsoft Word program, you may want to think about turning off the spell-check and editing function while you are writing. You don't need to be dictated to by computer programmers. They are not the best guides to good writing. Just turn it off. (Instructions can be found in "Miscellaneous Tips for Word" in Chapter 7, "Formatting Basics.")

If you haven't realized it yet, when you are writing in flow you are getting messy, and allowing things to be less than perfect. Perfectionism is the opposite of creativity, and it will stop flow in its tracks. Striving to be perfect activates the critic, and it also confines you, making you feel you can only put down what will stand for all eternity. What we really want is permission to be messy, and even bad. I call this kind of perfectionism the *Sufferings of Young Werthur* syndrome. *The Sufferings of Young Werthur* is a novel written by Goethe in 1774. It's about many things, including unrequited love, but what I got from it is that a young painter is distraught because what he paints is never as beautiful as the images he has in his head. In despair, he decides not to desecrate the images by putting them down on canvas, he just keeps them in his head. At the end of the book, he kills himself. What is Goethe's message?

Don't do that! That is, you need to know that *the very act of creation limits what you are creating.* The way I think of it is that the ideas artists get come from the ethers. Our job is to bring them down into form here on the physical plane. But the process of doing so inevitably limits or shrinks the original idea somewhat. It can never be in the physical world what it is in the ethers. The point is, it doesn't have to be. Great works of art are merely reflections, pointing people to that place in the ethers where the idea came from. And, doing so is enough; in fact it is heroic.

Commitment

Now, I want you to take a moment and make a commitment to yourself, one that's realistic, and one that you *believe* you can keep.

How many times can you show up to write this week? _____

How long can you write each time? ________________

And what do you want to work on when you first sit down?

____

(If this is hard, turn to Chapter 3, *Seducing the Muse*, and read about habits.)

Your homework is to write three pages. Don't try for more. Keep it simple. Under-commit, overachieve.

Chapter 2

Finding Your Voice

If you have always secretly wanted to write but haven't yet begun, one of the most intimidating acts is beginning to put words on the page. The first thing you will notice is, "but I didn't mean to sound like that!" You need to write for a while to find the "voice" you are meant to write with. What do I mean by a "voice?" It is the style with which you are writing. I am writing this book in a typical "how-to" style, which means I am simple, factual, and address the reader directly. I could have chosen to write this in a more academic style, which would mean I would write with authority and keep myself and personal stories out of it. Every writer has a style, and the more comfortable they are with it, and the more it suits what the material is, the better the voice and the better the writing.

The difficulty in finding your voice is that the best way to find it is to write, and if the sound of your own writing is making you cringe, it can be troublesome to get past this. But think about other things you have mastered. Cooking? Bike riding? Walking? Did you expect yourself to be able to do any of those things without practice? No. Then in order to find your writing self, you must free yourself to explore.

Maybe you are already well past the point of putting your first thoughts on paper, but you still may not have discovered your voice. You may be feeling confined by having to write as an expert, or you may be writing in an academic tone that doesn't feel like *you*; or, if you are writing a novel, you may not feel you have yet really captured the narrator.

It can feel frustrating to have to keep writing to uncover your voice. Especially if you are afraid everything you are writing will have to be discarded once you do uncover your voice. I want to encourage you to keep writing through this fear, because this is what writing *is*. There are many examples of writers consciously and deliberately choosing to discard what they've written once they find the way they actually want to tell the story. They know that all that time and all those words weren't wasted at all, because going through it was the only way to get down to the deeper place where they were writing from truth.

Here are two examples. First, Arthur Golden, the author of *Memoirs of a Geisha*, wrote two drafts of his book, one from the perspective of a male Western journalist, and one from a woman closer to the story, but not the geisha herself, before he had the courage to let himself take what he described as the "imaginative leap into the mind of the character." He had to risk writing from the perspective of the geisha herself. He feared writing about someone of the opposite sex *and* in a foreign culture, but once he trusted himself enough, it all came together. The book spent two years on the *New York Times* bestseller list, was translated into 32 languages and was made into a movie.

Frank McCourt, author of *Angela's Ashes*, rather famously taught high school English for almost 30 years while he worked intermittently on his memoir. It was only when he wrote from the voice of the child he had been that it came to life. He once explained in an interview, "After 20 pages of standard omniscient author, I wrote something that I thought was just a note to myself, about sitting on a seesaw in a playground, and I found my voice, the voice of a child." The child's voice had the rhythm of the speech, with the dialects, and most important, saw everything without judging it. *Angela's Ashes* went on to win the Pulitzer Prize and the National Book Critic's Circle Award, as well as selling four million copies in hardcover. It was also made into a movie.

A less famous story is that of my sister, whom I worked with throughout her first book, an allergy-free cookbook for kids. She kept complaining that she had no voice, until I asked her to imagine a parent that she had helped. "Imagine what you would say to her," I told her, "just write that down." For her, the key was who she was talking *to*.

For me, it took years of writing in my journal before I could write unself-consciously, which allowed me to write from my heart, and write simply, without worrying anymore about how it "sounded." I always wanted to sound complex and sophisticated, but no matter what I do, my sentences are simple and clear.

Here is an exercise to help you break through to your own voice. Set your timer for three minutes. Don't worry too much. You can answer it again a different way if you're not satisfied but do answer the question before you move on. Ready? Now. Answer this question:

Who are you, and why are you writing this book?

There are usually two different responses when I give this exercise in my classes. One is total fear and an inability to define "who I am." It can be challenging, because I am leaving it up to you to define yourself and you have to pick from all the identities you are, who it is who is writing. The second response is the one I hope for. It's when someone, even against their apparent will, steps up and states clearly who they are, why they and only they can write this book, and why the world needs to hear what they have to say. There are a million different ways people have answered the question. Some write what, typed out, could be the back cover copy for the book. One student wrote a poem. Most succeed in stepping away, at least temporarily, from that false humility society usually forces on us, and claim their power. They are assuming their own authority. This, to me, is what it means to find your voice. As an editor, I have had the experience many times of wading through pages of manuscript that seem okay, fine even, but not riveting, only to come upon a piece that would jump out at me. I would go back to the author and say, "You need to write more of *this*," and they would hesitate. "Oh, I didn't really *mean* that," they'd say. "I don't think I can really say it." But it's the heart of what they need to say.

What does it mean to find your voice? It is the moment when the truth leaps out of you – when you assume the authority to write. Writing demands authority. You can't be wishy-washy when you write if you want to write well. You can't wait for someone's permission. You need to tap into the source deep inside of you, the power hidden underneath politeness and deference and fear of being seen or causing trouble or being different. It is instantly recognizable. Suddenly, out of an endless flow of words will leap the core of the idea: the passionate, rich, loud voice.

What does it mean to develop your voice? It means you can embrace who you are, and accept and reveal your truth. Surprisingly, many people hesitate to write what they know in their hearts is the truth because it's not polite. We have it ingrained in us that we don't want to offend people. This doesn't make for good writing. When you are always trying to hide or cover up your meaning, the writing simply isn't clear and good.

What's really going on when you run into this problem is that you are trying to control how people will respond to what you write. You can't make everyone like you, and you can't make everyone like what you have to say or the way you are saying it. You have to let that go. In fact, trying to please in this way just makes the writing weak. We write what we write, and then let it go. Let others have their reaction, their response to it. That's not actually about you. Writing a book is a lot like having a child. You raise it and you give it the best you have, but at a certain point you let it go off into the world to have its own life and its own experiences.

You may have a particular reason to be concerned about others' reaction. It may not be people in general you are concerned about, but one person in particular. Frequently my students are writing about a real event—whether it's straight non-fiction, memoir, or fiction—and they know someone else has a different perspective on it, or doesn't want anyone at all talking about it, much less you.

It may be, for instance, that you are writing about a particular piece of history and your interpretation of events is radically different than that of the acknowledged expert on the subject. Or you might want to tell a specific story from your own life, and you know a family member doesn't want it revealed.

What I tell my students in these circumstances is, you can't write with someone hanging over your shoulder. You need to free yourself to write what *you* have to say. Then after you write it all out, you can decide whether you will keep all of it, part of it, or none in the final version. Free yourself to write now and decide later what to do with it. Writing it and publishing it (or even showing it to anyone) are two different things. In the most extreme version of this, you can think of Emily Dickenson. No one even knew she was a poet in her lifetime, but after she died all her writing was discovered beautifully tied up in ribbons waiting for the world to greet it.

I developed another exercise to help pinpoint what's going on in these circumstances. Ready? Set your timer again for another three minutes.

Who is it you want to hide this from?

It turns out that naming the person you are imagining criticizing you as you write can help free you. Now, at least you know what you are up against.

It could even be that you want to hide from yourself. You don't want to acknowledge or "own" that this is the truth, or this is your story, or this really happened.

There is a moment of truth for every writer: The moment when you claim your own story for you, and you write it the way you know it, and you lay out the truth the way you see it, without regard for another person's perspective, which may legitimately be different, and without regard for the effect it will have on other readers. This is what makes for good writing. It's not a moral decision. The moral decision can come later: what you will do with it.

Writing is an act of courage. It is also staking a claim on your view of the world. One thing I love about writing is that you have the floor, with no interruptions, and you can say things the way you see them.

Anne Lamott says if you experienced it, it's your story and no one can take it from you. If you had a bad divorce, it's great material, use it. And if you're worried about your ex-husband causing trouble, just give his character a really small penis, and he'll deny that it's him! Of course, Anne Lamott often takes things to the extreme. You may ultimately decide that there are certain things you won't say in the final book because you don't want to hurt people. All I'm saying is that if you try to do that *before* you begin writing, you are editing as you go, and therefore cutting off your flow. There are a couple of things that happen when you really free yourself to write out everything. One, you may discover a truth or a piece of information you didn't know before because you've given yourself the freedom to go in and retrieve it. Two, you may come out with a different perspective and realize that it is okay to say this after all.

If you are still struggling with this issue, you may want to look ahead to the exercise "Blocks Are Only There In Case You Want to Stop" in Chapter 3.

It will also help if you don't let anyone read this as you go along. There is power in keeping it to yourself. (An exception to that would be an even creative exchange, either with a writing buddy or in a safe writing group. See Appendix B. If everyone is risking sharing their creativity they understand and protect yours as well as their own.)

A question I am asked frequently is, should I write this story as memoir or fiction? What is the difference?

Well, truthfully, there's not always as much difference as people would like to think. *David Copperfield*, written in 1850, is pretty much true, according to Charles Dickens' biographers. And, as we now all know, *A Million Little Pieces* written by James Frey as memoir, was really fiction. The truth is, it can sometimes be easier to get at the truth by writing fiction. If you are freed entirely from the burden of writing what's literally true (this event did not really happen before that one, but it makes a better story), you can just get on with it and say what it is that has been burning up inside you. There can be an image or a piece of dialogue that never actually happened in quite that way, but when you put it down that way, it illuminates the truth.

So then, why write memoir at all? There's one very good reason: If it's important for the reader to know absolutely that this happened. Whether it's a particularly brutal rape as described in *Lucky* by Alice Sebold, or a horrific scene of war from *Born on the Fourth of July* by Ron Kovic, the writer needs the reader to know that this is a true event that forever changed the author, and the reader needs to know about it.

Remember, memoir is not autobiography, meaning, it's understood that your memory may be faulty, and the dialogue is not recorded, but you are doing your best, and you are not intentionally making stuff up, as Frey did.

Even if you aren't writing something about yourself, even if you are writing the most fact-based book imaginable—a handbook about the DMV, for instance—it will still reveal you. It is impossible for it not to. You will do better to accept that fact and be honest.

So, to make this as easy as possible, here's another exercise for you. Set your timer for three minutes. Ready?

What don't you want anyone to know?

What I can tell you for sure is that that piece, whatever it is, is probably essential to your story, or it will probably be revealed anyway. Going back to me for a second, even when I write non-fiction, I always wish I was complex and hard-boiled. Instead, what I almost always seem to reveal is that I am an optimist, I want to help people, and I can sometimes be extremely naïve. Once I accept that (and even tell you that directly), I don't have to write needlessly complicated sentences, or make events in my life seem worse than they are.

In the end, I believe that finding your voice really comes down to embracing who you are and accepting and revealing the truth.

Now, if you are writing a novel, there's another level you will need to reach. That is, each of your characters needs to have a voice, too. The very best writers are able to create characters so distinct that just hearing the dialogue, you know who is speaking. Think of Shakespeare and Jane Austen. Compare, for instance Bottom in *Midsummer Night's Dream* with Titania or Mrs. Bates in *Emma* with Mr. Woodhouse. In *Trainspotting*, Irvine Welsh creates separate voices for all his characters, so that Davie is distinct from Mark.

To do this properly, you will need to inhabit each character and let them speak. For a novelist, there is always a moment of truth, which is the moment when a character they have created and think they can control does something they don't expect or want. This to me signals you have succeeded as a novelist. Your characters are alive and just like people, they are not able to be controlled. If you can hang on and follow them where they lead,

I guarantee you will have a better novel. It may be very different from what you expected, but it will be alive.

If you don't do this, if you want to maintain control of your characters, you end up surrendering character development to plot, and in the extreme you wind up with cardboard characters like Nancy Drew or James Bond, who move through exciting, but obvious plots.

Exercise:

Interview your characters.

I mean this literally. Write a question on a pad and let the character answer it by using your non-dominant hand to answer. Give the character a chance to tell you who he or she is. Let them have the floor for awhile, and see what you learn.

Commitment:

Were you able to keep your commitment last week? If not, what did you do? What did you learn? What do you want to do differently?

How many times can you show up to write this week? _____

How long can you write each time? ________________

And what do you want to work on when you first sit down?

____

____

Again, your homework is to write three pages. Don't try for more. Keep it simple. Undercommit. Overachieve.

Chapter 3

Seducing the Muse

Getting started is one of the most difficult parts of writing. Sitting down and looking at that blank screen, or blank page, we can build up the pressure in our heads. All our fears of failure and fears of success paralyze us. Even writing one word, or one sentence, can be agony. It's sooo much easier to check emails, or wash the dishes. (There are many writers who have spotlessly clean houses. It's an easy way to keep busy but not do what we most want to do.) That's why daily habits are so important. Building a daily practice of writing takes a lot of the emotional charge out of it.

Here is an easy way to build that daily practice. Most writers I know say that once they get going, they enjoy the writing, and are very happy to *have* written. The biggest hurdle, in my experience, is getting through that space in between intending to write and actually writing: that is, the butt in the chair, fingers on the keyboard or pen, moving. We need a bridge to get us safely across from one space to the next. We need to avoid getting trapped in the fears that come up, which are really the voice of the Inner Critic:

I don't know how to write.

I have nothing to say.

It's boring.

I can't spell.

My grammar is bad.

I'm not writing in order.

What may be underneath:

It's not safe to tell the truth.

If I finish the book and it's published my friends will hate me.

If I finish the book and it's published and it gets a bad review in the *New York Times* I'll hate myself.

Once you are safely writing, it's like you've created a cocoon of creativity and flow, and the fears have been left behind. I find it helpful to think of it literally as a space, a place that I am going to. This is where habit comes in. Habits can be that bridge. We are creatures of habit, and we respond well to little rituals. I'm sure there are many rituals you perform throughout the day. Getting up and brushing your teeth. Having your morning coffee. A ritual like this creates a comfortable little groove we can slide into without thought. We just do it. What I want you to do is consciously create a little ritual that works for you to get you to the point where you are writing. Let me tell you mine. When I first started writing, I had an office on the ground floor of a two-story house. The kitchen and living room were upstairs. After I'd finished my breakfast and my morning routine, I put on a pot of tea—a special tea I didn't drink at any other time. It was particularly strong-smelling. (Everyone always wants to know what it was: Celestial Seasonings Bengal Spice.) When the tea was ready, I'd take it downstairs into my little office and sit with it in my hands as I turned on the computer and opened the file I was working on. I'd sit and think and take a sip or two. Then I'd put the cup down and begin typing. Now, there were many times that I didn't bring that tea down to start writing until 15, 10 or even 5 minutes before the end of my time. I showed up anyway and wrote for 5 minutes. The point is, the ritual began working. After awhile, I was making that same pot of tea, but, 9 times out of 10, I never even took a sip before my writing session was over because I started right in while the tea was still steeping, and plunged ahead. I became so engrossed I forgot all about it. As soon as I put the water on, my mind unconsciously began thinking of my writing, and I crossed the bridge to my writing space easily and effortlessly.

Some of my students light a candle at their writing desk before they begin. Several have a particular prayer or poem that they read. Some go for a walk before they start. Others go to the gym and exercise first. It doesn't matter what you do. Find the time, the space and the ritual that works for *you,* and begin.

Knowing the Right Time to Work

One thing I encourage my students to pay attention to is when their best time for writing might be. Everyone is different. As you commit to writing a certain amount each week, start to notice when it's easiest to do. Of course, your schedule does depend on what goes on in your life right now, and your best time might not be available. But if you focus on it, things might shift too. For instance, you might like writing best first thing in the morning after you wake up. Or, you might prefer night time after your kids are in bed. Maybe you like the openness of a weekend to write during the day. I have always preferred writing in the morning before I really begin my day. (That means no checking email or answering the phone till I'm done.) But in the past five years, while my daughter has been little, I can't do that. I have had to write when she naps (I have become very familiar with McDonald's parking lots when she falls asleep in the car—they are brightly lit), or when friends could watch her for me. It might not be as simple as my old schedule, but it works.

One of my students used to write every morning on the ferry in to work. Later when he moved and needed to take the bus, he was actually able to maintain his focus and write on the bus too. (That's dedication!) Another student woke at four in the morning and wrote. This meant she was in bed pretty early too, but it worked for her.

I am never surprised when students tell me they wake up at three a.m. with an idea. I don't know why, but it seems a common phenomenon when your creativity is engaged. It might just be that your subconscious has a chance to work. I only know it happens often. Keep a pen and paper and flashlight by your bed so you can jot your ideas down and get back to sleep! I have heard it said that the veil between the worlds (or between us and the ethers) is thinnest then. I do know it's true that late night or early morning is quieter, and there's less energy of distraction in the air. I think that's why many prefer these times.

Where to Write

Another thing to pay attention to is *where* you write. Do you have a place set aside in your house just for writing? Are you trying to write at the same desk where you do your work or pay your bills? Are you trying to write in a room your family needs to walk through? Does your family interrupt you the minute you sit down?

Of course, all writers would love to have the "Room of One's Own" that Virginia Woolf wrote about. (By the way, she had not a room but a whole separate cottage in the back yard for writing.) But it is possible to write consistently without one. Laptops have become invaluable for this. It means you really can write anywhere. Some students prefer getting out and writing in a café. Being around people can be comforting, and the noise can become a hum in the background as you focus, and you are prevented from distracting yourself with housekeeping chores. For some reason, many women tell me if their husband is in the house they cannot write at all. (And so far it does seem to be only women who have issues with men, not the other way around.) Others find it best to remove themselves from where the kids are, so they can't knock on the door.

I have had several writers tell me they prefer to write in their cars. One student used to sit in her car in the parking lot and write for an hour before writing class started. Another student took advantage of having no wifi to distract her in the car, and she drove somewhere with a pretty view for each writing session.

If you do want to write at home and can't have a separate space just for writing, think about using another ritual and/or some talisman to help you shift your space. Maybe you can set out a picture of your favorite author or set all the work papers aside, or have a special bulletin board with just writing-related things posted. One student used the trick of draping a tablecloth over his other work so it wasn't visible to him.

Take the time to get the supplies you need. The laptop if you can. Good pens and notebooks. Maybe a nice bag to carry your things in, if you write outside of the house–your ritual items if you have them (candle, cloth, special totems).

The other element that can be crucial to having a daily practice is to write continuously when you do begin to write. Just as a large sailing ship takes a long time to get going, so does your writing. It's much easier to keep going than it is to move from a standing start. How much or how frequently you will need to write to keep in motion is entirely up to you. I have some students who swear by the writing-every-day method—no matter how much time they write, by writing at least something every day, they stay immersed in their subject matter or with their characters. Other people write only five days a week and take the weekend off. Some people can only write on weekends, but they write every weekend. I've never written more than three hours a week except on one occasion when I was finishing a book and wrote five days a week for a month. But three days a week is enough for me to stay immersed. I've even found now that I'm a mom, once a week can work for me. The key is, you have to make writing your top priority, and commit to your schedule no matter what it is—keeping in mind that this, your highest priority, may not take up the most time. Even fifteen minutes a day can move us forward in our writing. I know some writers (mostly novelists) who find showing up fifteen minutes each day to be the most useful commitment. It keeps them in touch with their characters daily, and it's a manageable amount of time. Almost all of us can come up with fifteen minutes. You can even do that while waiting in the line to pick up your child from school, or while your car is being serviced.

I find that the key to making the best use of small segments of time is to be able to drop quickly into that special space we all create when we are in the flow of our writing. This is the reason I have been able to write whole books while putting in very little time. I'm really good at getting across the bridge and right down into my creative space. Since becoming a mom, I find this has actually gotten easier for me. (No time to procrastinate. When the sitter is there, I get to work!) But I have always been religious about using certain tools to help me quickly cross the bridge from my day-to-day reality into my creative space. Making the commitment actually helps. When I first began this, I would often procrastinate for fifty minutes of my hour—but I'd show up for the last ten. Gradually, I learned how to jump in and make progress, and persevere. Of course, this is where the students in the writing classes help each other. We don't want to show up the following week without having done what we said we would do! You can do this yourselves by finding a writing buddy to check in with weekly on your individual commitments. (See Appendix B.)

Another trick that helps you stay immersed in your writing is leaving yourself something to write at the end of your writing time. Don't write yourself dry. Leave a little bit for the next time. I sometimes write notes to myself about what I want to start with when I come back. In one of her novels, Barbara Pym, an English novelist, had a character who was herself a writer. She would always leave the page in the typewriter at the point of the last sentence she wrote, so she could just jump right back in again. I will usually say something like this:

> [From here I want to go to the material on
> fears, and then Seducing the Muse]

It can also be helpful to avoid rereading everything you wrote before. That can put you into editing mode very quickly, with your inner critic likely right behind, ready to pounce. If you've left a marker for yourself like a bracket, you can skip right to where you left off by searching for the bracket. (See Chapter 7, "Formatting Basics" for more Microsoft Word hints.)

All these tricks make it easier to bridge the gap and get back into your writing space. Remember that the antidote to all the fears is to write! It takes you into the creative space where the creative voice is louder than the critical voices. It's really the *only* thing that works.

Seducing the Muse

I tell people you have to think of that creative part of you, the part that is in touch with the deepest dreams and visions you are trying to express, as your date. She is a woman, of course (the creative part of us is feminine), and she's finicky. You have to seduce her. What would you do if you were trying to get someone to go out with you? (Or, what would you want someone to do for you?) You'd get flowers, chocolates, you'd dress in a way that pleased her. You'd be on time. This is what you have to do for your muse. I have one client who was spending a lot of time cleaning her house, and not getting any writing done. I told her she might be looking at it wrong. It seemed that her muse needed things a certain way before she was willing to come out. I had her make a list of things her muse wanted. It was a very long list, and it included an orderly workspace, with flowers on the table. Not everyone's muse will have those requirements. My muse actually doesn't require neatness at all. She does require a specific space in the house (not a whole room, but a place where this happens and only this). She also will leave if I start to get caught up in any "work" activity, like answering emails or taking phone calls. She likes it best if I have a very quiet morning, then go for a long walk, and then show up to write immediately. Also, I have to keep writing in my journal close to every day (although it doesn't necessarily connect with whatever project it is that I'm writing).

What does your muse require?

Your muse is also like a date in that she will respond to consistency. If you keep showing her that you are showing up for her, she will show up for you too. It may take awhile for this to happen. Once you've made the connection (just like with a date) you may not have to go as all out each time. You may be startled by a big creative burst. You might produce twice as much material as usual, or get a sudden inspiration on how to solve a plot point, or receive insight you hadn't before. You might get ideas for other books. (If this happens, "harvest" the ideas and set them aside for later. See the next section for more.)

As you begin to trust your muse more, you will more easily end your writing sessions when your time is up, because you trust that she will be there again when you return in your next scheduled time.

Harvesting Creativity

When you are working with creativity, and you begin to really harness it, you may find yourself bubbling over with other ideas. I had one client who felt like she was being undisciplined about reaching her goal of completing her novel because she wasn't writing it, and found herself thinking about a short story idea she had. As we talked about it, and I made this suggestion to her, she confessed that she actually had a whole book idea of short stories in her head. She happened to be the mother of three, the youngest just a year old. I asked her if when her son was born she loved her daughters any less. "No," she laughed. "There was just more love to go around."

"Creativity is like that," I said. "Creativity begets more creativity. You can't hurt your first writing project by having a new idea." I also pointed out that trying to force herself to focus only on the original idea without letting the new one out had ended up blocking her (she hadn't written in two weeks). I encouraged her to go ahead and let herself write out what she had in her head. Once she had done that (unblocked the dam) I knew the force of the flow would help her get back to her first project.

Of course, sometimes people do end up putting one project aside if another comes up and is more pressing. There's a woman in one of my classes who came in thinking she was going to write a memoir about a specific event in her life. She was struggling with that for a few months. Then one day she came in with a fragment that was an idea she had for a novel. She was just playing with it. We loved it! Week after week she came in with more pages, more details on characters, and it was easy and fun. We all encouraged her to keep going, and trust that when the time was right she would get back to that other project.

I confess I have never written only one book at a time. I am almost always actively working on two. For a long time I was writing my memoir twice a week and once a week I wrote on my time book. Then as things heated up with it, I switched and focused only on it until it was done. Then I went back to the memoir and this book. I know that as I get closer to the end I will turn my attention fully onto this project as well.

Having said that, the other thing you need to do is focus on only one or two as your main projects. As other ideas come up, take them seriously, write them down. (It's good to get in the habit of carrying a pen and a small pad with you everywhere, using your cell phone or, like Anne Lamott, carry just a pencil and an index card with you.) Create real files for them labeled properly on your computer or in your file cabinet. Honor them. And then turn back to your main project.

How to Keep Going

OK, I've been showing up, and I've been writing, but it's not good and it doesn't mean anything. So I guess I'll stop now.

Don't do it! This is the key point: Continuing on. You've gotten through the hard part. You started. Now use the momentum to keep going. This is where being among a group of supportive writers can be helpful. I see this happening with my classes all the time. I can't tell you how many people have told me, "As soon as I stopped going to class, I stopped writing. So I came back." You may want to refer to "How to Start a Writing Group That Works" in Appendix B for support.

Because I've worked on so many books, I really know that they do start this way. All messy and incoherent, or maybe a really good outline and some jotted notes, or maybe even just a good title, or something written on a scrap of paper. We've all had that. Now the trick is to keep going with it. If you think of really successful creative people (and I define successful creativity as creativity that expresses itself), they keep going. They believe or know that this is the way it works. I love a story I heard Billy Crystal tell once on TV. He was watching a travel program, and he had an idea. He said he wrote it down immediately on a pad–and note that he has pads all over his house! He knows how to harvest his creativity. The idea was, a couple of guys, midlife crisis, go to a dude ranch. That was it. That was all he wrote down. That idea became *City Slickers.* It would never have come to fruition if he had not harvested the idea, started writing and kept going. Of course, being Billy Crystal, he was able to have a meeting with someone that led to the deal before he wrote, but he knew to follow through. (In fact, follow-through is how he became successful in the first place.) He had faith in the process.

Blocks Are Only There In Case You Want to Stop

There's another way to look at blocks, and I've found it very freeing. I have adapted this exercise from a book called *Beyond Visualization* by Viki King (New World Library, 1992). Try doing it first without reading further. Here's how. Take a blank piece of paper and draw a horizontal line all the way across it:

Now mark an X on the far right end. This is your goal. For our purposes I want you to label it either "Manuscript completed" or "Book published." It doesn't really matter which. Now put an X somewhere on that line to represent where you feel you are now in relation to that goal. Don't think about it too much. This is an intuitive, not a literal, exercise. Then, mark as many X's on the line as you think you need to get to the goal. You may put in fifty tiny X's between the two, or perhaps you only need three big ones. The point is, most people get stuck because they immediately jump ahead from the X where they are to the X at the very end. This frightens them so much that they run back to the first X and stop completely. But the X's are actually there to *help you get ready* to get to the last X. You only need to go from the first X to the second X and stop there. (To really drive this point home for yourself, you can insert a long, dark vertical line between the second and third X's.)

XX|XXXXXXXXXXXXXXXXX

When you let yourself complete that first step, something amazing happens. You change. You become ready to proceed to the next X. And you can take as long as you like at each X, or even decide half way through to change your goal and not continue along this line. That's OK. The point is to become aware that you are on a path, and focusing on the next step without worrying about the one after actually allows you to proceed without fear. Because you also know that *blocks (represented by all those X's) are only there in case you want to stop.* By the time you get to the end, you will find (especially if you are one who had 50 X's) that the last step is no longer frightening at all.

By the way, don't try to get too literal and start labeling all the X's. It's not really about that, it's about letting yourself become conscious of your fears instead of paralyzed by them. You may find if you let yourself do the exercise a second time in a few weeks, you won't have as many X's because you have already become less afraid. Just keep going from one X to another.

A River of Creativity

When it's feeling difficult to show up, or you are feeling that you are not making any progress, it can be helpful to keep in mind that creativity has an ebb and a flow. Sometimes it seems like you can only get out a sentence or a paragraph in an hour, and you find yourself compulsively figuring that at this rate, your book will take twenty years. You are in the ebb. If you hold on, and stay committed, you will be shocked and surprised when the flow comes back and you can write twenty pages in an hour.

It's a very fine line between showing up in your writing time and thinking that you have to produce. That's why I often encourage people not to keep track of how much they write. Sometimes you produce a lot and sometimes you produce a little. It's not linear. You can control the time you show up but not the amount you produce, so don't pressure yourself in that way.

I find myself saying to students over and over that this is what writing is. And sticking with it through the tougher parts is the hardest and most important thing for a writer to do.

I remember having that feeling when writing my first book. Every sentence I wrote seemed cobbled together, just putting facts down unimaginatively. Then the flow returned, and I was on a high again, loving what I wrote. Later, when I was putting the chapter together, I looked at those sentences that were so hard and they didn't seem so out of place. Still later, I could no longer recognize which were the hard ones and which the flow ones. I realized that my judgment and perspective had been off in the ebb.

Another thing to keep in mind is that these sentences, paragraphs and pages add up to chapters, and chapters add up to books. This is the way writing gets done.

Creativity is like a river. When you're too stuck in the controlling, trying-to-produce side of things, it's like you are trying to dam the river. You want to be able to stop it, and predict what it will do. But rivers don't do well like that. They need to flow. Sometimes there's eddies, or slack places, but the river is always flowing. If you've been stuck, you may need to get back into the river.

I had a client who was very meticulous and orderly by nature, and she also had some strong voices telling her she needed to produce in a neat and structured way. Of course that's not how creativity works and she knew that. She'd been writing along very successfully when she found herself stuck again. Somehow, without knowing it, she'd succumbed again to the idea that she had to produce.

It got so bad that the only cure for her was to give herself an entire month off from writing. Not only that, she took time away for a weekend in the mountains, and she literally got into a river. That's what it took for her to reconnect with her flow.

I know in our culture everyone has this fantasy: "If I could just go away for a couple weeks" or a month or six months or a year. People think they need to be out of their daily lives and far away in order to write. And I know that that's not true. In fact, in my observation, it can sometimes be harder to write when you have open time like that. Expectations can become high. You can feel pressured. Even a clear schedule can make it harder to write. I know that sounds crazy. But the people I've worked with who have had zero issues with procrastination have been mothers of children under five. When you have absolutely no time, you just get down to business! When I came back from my maternity leave, I could only write once a week for two hours, sometimes only one. Yet I felt immersed in my writing and could see the progress I was making, even though it was slower than I wanted. The fault lies in the black-and-white thinking: "I need four hours to make a difference at all in my writing." "I need a whole day to get this concept out." "I need a whole week to get this done." "If I could just get a month off, then the novel would be finished!" In fact, incremental consistent progress does get a book done.

Giving yourself completion points can help when it gets hard. Studies have proven that small frequent rewards for achievement help the most in keeping us on track. Celebrating each marker can help you see your progress, and rewards can help you keep going. A good starting point is acknowledging when you show up for your writing time. My students get a gold star each week for this. You can then move on to bigger things like a scene sketched out, a specific number of pages or a chapter completed. We'll be talking more about completion points in Chapter 4, "Structure"

It's so important in the beginning to be careful what you say to others out in the world. What you want to avoid is that dreaded question, "How's your book coming?" followed by "You mean you aren't done yet?" Most people out in the world don't realize what is entailed in actually completing a book. And even some fellow writers aren't very generous. Set expectations low, and enjoy the process, in your own time, every step of the way.

Commitment:

It starts with a commitment. Were you able to keep your commitment last week? If not, what did you do? What did you learn? What do you want to do differently?

Now, keeping all that in mind, your homework is to write three pages. Can you commit to a definite time this week when you will show up?

How many times can you show up to write this week? _____

How long can you write each time? ________________

And what do you want to work on when you first sit down?

____

____

Remember, undercommit. Overachieve.

Chapter 4 

Structure

Many writers, once they've gotten past the dreaded beginning, find writing in flow to be fun and absorbing for a time. They aren't even particularly thinking too much about where they are headed, they are so relieved to be writing and beginning to accumulate pages. Invariably, one day, a student will come into my class with a stack of pages, anywhere from 50 to 100, in frustration. "I need to get this organized," they will say. I call it the binder stage. I encourage my students, when they are ready, to get a binder to begin organizing their work. This is the beginning of structure, the necessary component to finishing your book.

How do you know when you are ready?

The best way I can describe it is that an urge comes over you. It's like a pregnant woman suddenly needing to arrange the baby's room in the ninth month. You can't stand it anymore, just writing and writing without knowing where you are going. You will also know when you find everything I say in this chapter to be incredibly helpful. If you don't understand it at all, or if you end up buying a binder and lots of separators, but never do anything with it, you are just not ready yet. Go back and enjoy writing in flow. On the other hand, if you know it's time but you still aren't doing it, do it with a witness. Find someone to just sit with you as you put pages in the binder. Also it helps to remember that this level of structure does not have to be final. There will be plenty of opportunities to rearrange and refine what you do. The important thing is to create enough structure now so you can keep going.

It's natural not to think that much about structure at first (beyond knowing the general direction you are headed, perhaps being sure about your ending but not clear on how to get there). And second, when you are ready to think about it, you are really ready. When that moment comes, here are some tips to help you. First, the binder. Why do I always recommend a binder? Because it's tangible, and it's an easy visual way to sort things. Also, it's another step to giving your work form. People are always surprised when they print it out, how much material they've already written. I find that writing only on the computer without printing actually hurts form—it's really a never-ending scroll.

Binder Organization

One of the benefits of being in classes with others is you get to see how others organize their stuff. There's a friendly competition in my classes over binders. You can get quite obsessed, in a good way. Here are some basics:

Start printing on three-hole-punch paper, and don't forget to use headers or footers (see Chapter 7, "Formatting Basics"), which will name every page by title, page number and also date printed.

If you have definite chapters, and you know what most of them are, use tabs to separate into the chapters, as well as creating an additional catch-all for pieces you can't yet place, another tab for the outline, and a tab for the introduction.

My binder for this book contains these headers:

Outline;

Chapter 1: Where Are You Stuck?;

Chapter 2: Finding Your Voice;

Chapter 3: Seducing the Muse;

Chapter 4: Structure;

Chapter 5: Editing Your First Draft;

Chapter 6: How Do You Know When You Are Done?;

Chapter 7: Formatting Basics;

Chapter 8: Publishing;

Chapter 9: What's Next;

Conclusion;

Section called Previous Draft

If you are writing a memoir, it might be helpful to have these:

List of memories you want to include

Sections for each of certain periods of time (Childhood, Young Adult, Early Adult, Later)

If you are writing fiction, and you don't yet know your chapters, you might want to have a tab for each character and include everything you know about them in it, a tab for a timeline of events, a tab for current writing, and a tab for all the writing to date.

Why is this helpful?

First, as I said, it gives you a sense of how much you have. Second, it's helpful to be able to flip through quickly and scan material. It's also easy to write notes on, and to read aloud. But I find that the act of organizing what you have in this way spurs you on to think of things you hadn't before, sections you will need for this particular book.

You will still be writing in flow even when you have set up your binder. You are able to capture ideas and it doesn't matter what order they are in. As long as you jot down the material, you can accept that you can figure it out later. And when you are writing in flow, that is magic. But then the moment occurs when it is no longer possible to write this way. Why is it no longer possible? Most likely, you've already written out all the separate pieces of flow that can be written. It's like putting together a quilt. You have all your pieces chosen and cut out. At a certain point you need to begin arranging them and stitching them together. Or you may not have finished all the pieces, but you can't avoid realizing that the reader will need to take in thing one before they can move on to understanding thing two. And you need to understand how to make this happen in order to keep going. Sometimes each piece of writing is discrete and will not change no matter the order. But other times, the order is crucial. A murder mystery is the obvious case in point. If you don't know certain clues, you won't be able to figure it out.

Here's how I approach it in class. I'm going to give you an exercise to do, and you will hate it. I'm going to give you six minutes. Ready? Set your timers. Write off the top of your head what the outline is. Don't go looking on your computer, don't go get the last outline you may have written. Do it right here, cold, on a piece of paper. When you force yourself, you will put something down, and you might reveal something you didn't see before. If you are a novelist, it may be easier to think of this as a map of the territory rather than an outline. Think of what you know now, and where you want to end up. Write it here.

If you find 6 minutes isn't enough, double the time.

I will tell you that I have always done this exercise with my students in class, and I discovered the right structure for my time book and my memoir this way, completely unexpectedly.

In class, what I do next is put the structure up on the board. I usually demonstrate with one fiction and one non-fiction outline. The capacity to picture your book visually will help you to see what you have, and give you insight about what you *don't* have, or what you have too much of. When people get stuck they tend to narrow down, and literally can't see the big picture. They need to be pulled out of their narrow focus. These different ways to look at structure can be very effective at that.

So how can you throw your plot, or what you know of it, or your structure, up on the board? Let's start simply. If you have a white board and want to use it, that's fine; but, I'd recommend getting big Post-it paper (they make super large pads of it) so that you can save your work. Make sure you have at least four colored markers, too.

Now, make a timeline. Most all books, fiction and nonfiction, have a timeline as a basic structure. If you know already that there are three timelines because it is a multi-generational story, stack three different colored lines on top of each other, leaving space between. Then, start filling in the dates of events as you know them. If you don't know specific dates yet, you can take a guess, or you can stop and think through what you want them to be. Or, leave some or all of them blank for now, and just have events in the correct order but without exact dates. You can use different colors for different characters or themes.

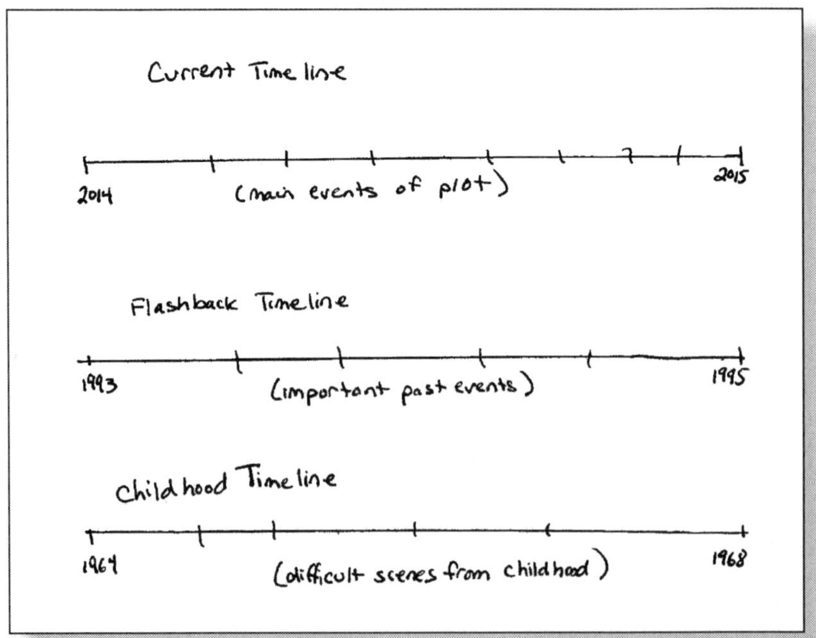

One of my students went home after I used this technique on another student in her class, and created three timelines, one for each character, in three different colors.

Even though she'd almost finished her manuscript, by doing this she was able to put down a few things she hadn't yet made concrete, and it helped her finish her story (not to mention plot the next two books in the series).

You might immediately realize a problem, like another one of my students. She had started writing, as many creative writers do, with scenes, dialogue, a piece of the plot, and hadn't thought it all through (which is *good*. She was in the harvesting ideas place). So when I wanted to put her timeline up, I asked what I always ask: Where does the story start? This wasn't a trick question. The opening scene of the book is mysterious—a woman on a train. We hear her inner monologue but aren't sure who she is or where she is going to or from. A good beginning. But then I said, "So does the story start a week before?" She realized in one version it starts ten years before, and in another, it was a month earlier. So I ended up giving her three big post-it pages each with a different character's timeline of events. She was to mark all the events she knew for each, and then look at how to tell the story. She'd never seen visually how each character's events overlapped, and it was a breakthrough.

If the timeline isn't working at all for you, you may need to arrange things by subject (this would probably work for nonfiction). See if there is still a sequence (*this* has to be understood before *that*) or if the order is not significant and it all is interchangeable.

Instead of chronologically or by subject, you may want to think about structuring your book by the progression of emotional flow. This can work well for narrative non-fiction, or memoir, and is also how many novels are organized. Look at where the emotional peak of the story is. The story flows according to emotional impact until it reaches a crescendo. In order to have that effect, you may need to deliberately go against the timeline—reveal information out of order. Often the peak moment, or revelation, may be something that happened in the character's very early childhood—and if the story was told in order, that effect would be totally lost.

Catch-22 is a classic example of a story following an emotional—not a chronological—arc. The event that colors Yossarian's life and hovers around the entire story, happened before the chronology of the story starts, but isn't revealed until almost the end.

A basic peak structure would have emotional tension hitting certain points until the crescendo, and then ending.

or building slowly to the big moment, and then ending

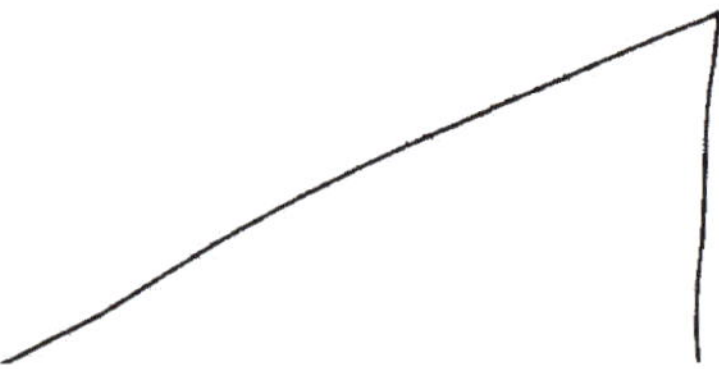

The more traditional structure with the pinnacle occurring in the middle of the story can also feel less exciting.

If you are writing fiction or memoir, you may find it interesting to note that there aren't actually all that many plots to work from. Remember that Shakespeare never (or hardly ever) made up his own plots. He stole them from other people's work. The point is never just the plot itself. To that end, I must recommend a book that I dearly love, *The Seven Basic Plots* by Christopher Booker (Continuum, 2009). I think it's brilliant, and the definitive work on the subject (although there are many out there). Here are his seven:

* Overcoming the Monster (think *Jaws*)
* Rags to Riches (*David Copperfield)*
* The Quest (*The Odyssey*)
* Voyage and Return (*Alice in Wonderland*)
* Comedy *(*In the classic sense, which refers to having a happy ending — any Jane Austen will do.*)*
* Tragedy (*Macbeth*)
* Rebirth (*A Christmas Carol*)

There's much more to the book than this, but this is a taste to help you to think of what your underlying story is. I know that it is especially useful if you are writing a memoir and need to take real life and impose a structure on it. For instance, you may not have realized that your story follows the same rough outline as the Rebirth plot. Reviewing the classic plot may help you in deciding what to focus on and what to leave out.

Sometimes what you will immediately see when you try to write the outline on a timeline is that it has become unwieldy and you have too much material. This is very common. People writing their first book (especially if it's nonfiction) tend to put in every idea they've ever had--partly out of enthusiasm, and partly out of fear that they'll never have another opportunity. But you will, especially if you do what you can to make this book good! It can be a big relief to realize that the reason you've been wrestling with the material, or have even gotten completely stuck, is because you are trying to include something you don't even need. Don't worry though, the material you don't need in this book could very well be the basis for your next work. It's hard sometimes to admit how narrow and simple your final book will need to be.

I was working with one writer who was writing a deep, complex book about the thinking of a historical figure. He had always planned on writing the biography of the figure's early years in the beginning, but kept getting stuck when he tried to write it. Finally, he realized that what he was writing was *not* a biography, and he was elated to realize he didn't need to write those chapters; in fact, the book was enhanced by leaving out what was boring to him. (Remember that if it bores you, it will probably bore the reader too.)

I had another client who was writing a memoir. She had a large cast of very colorful characters around her and was struggling to find the end to her story. It wasn't until she realized that she didn't have to tell her *whole* life story, that she could focus more narrowly on one particularly harrowing thread, that she was able to find the ending.

The beauty of letting go of saying *everything* is that you then have one specific thing that will actually better convey what you have to say. Letting go of every potential option leaves you with the one choice: the book that says what you want to say *now*.

I always tell my students that when you begin writing a book, you have endless possibilities in front of you. It's like the opening of a "V." When you are writing in flow with endless possibility you can choose one thread and follow it, and the next day land somewhere else and follow another thread. There are millions of different ways your story can go. But as you get further in, the choices constrict until ultimately you are looking at a narrow opening where all that is left is *one* thread or *one* path. It can feel like you have to place your foot exactly on the right spot—like there's only one way through this narrow channel and if you place your foot wrong, you will fail. It's easy to get caught up in perfectionism here and let the critic take over again and run rampant. In fact, this is the point at which many writers get stuck. There is another way to look at it however, which I hope will help you see it differently (and make your critic go back to the corner of your office again).

Flow vs. Structure

This is flow versus structure, and I believe the tension between the two is where creativity occurs. Another way to think of it is in psychological terms. The Myers-Briggs Type Indicator is a system of categorizing kinds of differences in people. The last of the four areas with two options in each is "perceiving" vs. "judging." A perceiving type prefers having all options constantly available, a judging type prefers having decisions made and set. Ideally, everyone would have a balance of both. If you make a decision too soon, without all the information you need, it may not be a good decision. If you keep postponing decisions, you will never get anywhere. So, the way I look at it is, in the beginning stages of writing a book, the best way to function is as a perceiving type—loose, flexible, open to all possibilities. At the end of writing a book, the best way to function is as a judging type: decisive and clear and in a set path. If you are too judging in the beginning the book might be too narrow and dry; if you are too perceiving at the end you might never complete the book because you are unwilling to give up having *every* possibility in order to have the *one* choice.

I think this is what happens with the students I've worked with who complained that they were great at starting projects but never finished any. They had fun at the beginning but when they got to this part, where the choices narrowed, they stopped.

So if that's you (and if structure is giving you problems, it may very well be you), below are some ideas and examples to help you improve your judging function when you are working on the end of the book.

Write What You Know

I had one student tell me in her first class that she had written the beginning of her mystery, and she knew the end, but was struggling with the middle. When she'd gone as far as she could from the front end, I suggested she skip to the end and write what she knew there. She did that, and then kept writing backwards and forwards until she understood what *needed* to be in the middle, and she was done. If that is an option for you, it can be very helpful to skip where you are stuck and write from where you know you want to get to. What it does is help illuminate the path that will lead you from one place to the other. It helps narrow down your choices. This can work even if it's not the end that you know, but just a place further along. (And by the way this can work for both fiction and non-fiction.)

The most amazing story I can share with you of writing out

what you know first is that of my student Blanca Florido who was writing a novel. She told us one day how when she got an idea for a scene and didn't know where to put it, she'd simply skipped ahead in her notebook (she was writing long-hand) and written it there. She thought no more about it, and continued writing from where she had left off. A few weeks later, just when she realized she'd gotten to a place in her story where that scene would fit perfectly, she turned the page and there it was.

Focus on Your Reader

Another way to let go of some possibilities is to think about how you want your readers to feel when they close the book. What is the most important message you are trying to convey? Write that down. Now, how best can you get them there? What is the most elegant and efficient way? Pretend you are the captain of a ship in the middle of the ocean, and your destination is the tiny island, which is where you want your reader to land. What are the co-ordinates? What is the best route to steer the ship?

Ask Your Characters

If you are writing fiction, and you are still not sure of the ending, another technique is to ask your characters. You may find that they know more than you do. Here's how to do this. First, pick a character. It could be your main character or it could be an ancillary character who knows more. Then, give yourself a quiet place with pen and paper. Now write your first question out with your dominant hand, and let your character answer, writing with your non-dominant hand. It may feel silly, and you may think you are making it all up—and actually, the truth is, you are. This is just a technique to help you access parts of your subconscious, which is where your writing comes from anyway. Keep an open mind, and see what happens. I had a client try this technique, and she reported back to me the following week that her main character knew everything that was going to happen!

Let Yourself Have Contained Flow

Now, once you've figured out where you are going, or you know where you want to focus next, it can also be helpful to give yourself a little feeling of flow within that structure. Often, at this point, people are writing at the bottom of a very long file or in the middle of a chapter. This can create the feeling of constriction that can tip you into an editing mode before you're ready, with the critic leaning over your shoulder. "Now that you know where you are going, you can't mess it up!" she says. A very simple technique to use in this situation is to give yourself permission to open a brand-new document or handwrite on a new pad. Write the section or scene out with the freedom to be messy. When you are done, you can put it back where it belongs.

Try Different Options

It's possible that you are still caught in that feeling of constriction and can't get out of it. Maybe you had really enjoyed writing in flow and miss that feeling of easy creativity. I hope you can see now why some narrowing is necessary, but constriction is not. Instead of focusing on the "right" choice, or the right place to put your foot, free yourself by thinking of the story as water flowing down a hill. Just go down the easiest, most fun way. Then, when you've hit the bottom, if you don't like where you've arrived, go back up to that last point and try coming down another way. Make it playful.

Research

Research is a favorite way to hide or not finish a book. Usually it's fear, fear of not knowing enough, or being criticized by others who do. I once worked with an author who'd received a healthy advance from a publisher to write a popular book on the subject she taught her (mostly corporate) clients. She hired me because she was gripped with fear about not being able to write in a way that would be respected in the academic field. Even though she knew that what she had been paid to write was a popular book, and she really didn't need any more research than she'd already done, it was very difficult to let go of the feeling that she had to please those academics who might one day read the book.

In areas where research seems required, I usually recommend (unless you are actually a historian or a journalist) that you write everything you know off the top of your head first, creating brackets and putting a note to yourself whenever you need to look up a piece of information or a fact.

Only when you have completely outlined all you have to say should you go back and create the list of what you need to look up. Then give yourself a time limit, and begin. If you find there's a whole body of material you didn't know about, ask yourself a few key questions:

1. Do I really need to know this for the book?
2. Could this be another book?
3. Does my audience really care about this?
4. How thorough do I need to be?
5. Is there someone I'm trying to impress or please? Is there someone I'm trying to protect myself from? Do I need to?

If you are really convinced you need to research, give yourself time limits and keep asking these questions periodically.

If you are in fact a historian or a journalist, you will have to begin with research, and form your ideas and writing after you have discovered the thread of your story within it. If you impose the story on the research first, you may close yourself off from new information. You may still want to set time limits on the research, and write up notes from what you are thinking as you go along. Once you have completed the initial research, you can follow the approach suggested above of writing out the story, and filling in research as needed. Be aware though that for most journalists and historians, research can be a seductive trap. There will always be more research that can be done; at a certain point you simply have to stop.

When people get stuck they tend to narrow down, and they need to be pulled back to the big picture. These different ways to look at structure can be very effective at giving you a new perspective. I have come to trust that when writers are working deeply on the structure, things begin to sort themselves out clearly. A coaching client told me one day how she'd finally decided not to worry so much about the various pieces of her story and how everything was going to fit. Then, when she started to review the material, she kept coming to a place and saying, "Oh, this material can go in here, and that material can go there." It all fit together easily.

Commitment:

Wherever you are with your structure, commitment is still what's needed. Were you able to keep your commitment last week? If not, what did you do? What did you learn? What do you want to do differently?

Now, keeping all that in mind, your homework is to write three pages. Can you commit to a definite time this week when you will show up?

How many times can you show up to write this week? _____

How long can you write each time? ________________

And what do you want to work on when you first sit down?

____

____

Remember, undercommit. Overachieve.

Chapter 5

Editing Your First Draft

You've finished the first draft. You've followed instructions, so you were writing in flow without editing and you know there are a lot of things to fix. Some things you know are just messy and need tightening, some things are out of order, some you just aren't sure of. Or, you haven't followed instructions. Half your manuscript has had some editing, and half hasn't. Either way, how should you approach the first round of editing?

There is a particular order to follow now. It will insure that you don't waste time or duplicate any work. You are going to start with the big, sweeping, structural changes, and move down from there to the level of paragraph, then sentence, and finally, word choice.

If you find yourself totally intimidated here, and the critic's voice is starting to pop up, you are probably not yet ready for this chapter. You may want to go back and re-read chapters 1 – 4. This chapter will be here when you are ready for it. No need to rush it.

If you made an agreement with your inner critic (see the sample Inner Critic contract in Chapter 1), this is the time you most likely agreed to let the critic have a say. Here's the big secret. You now have a healthy editor to step in and not permit the critic to attack you personally, or create excuses so that you never finish. It's not that you are ignoring the critic, it's that the critic is now part of the whole, not the only voice you listen to. You now have positive voices as well.

You are probably also worrying because you thought you were done but you know you have so much more to do, so you aren't sure whether you are entitled to celebrate. There are always stages to "doneness," and it helps to realize that there are at least seven completion points.

The Seven Completion Points to Finishing a Book

* The first done point is, of course, when you get the whole story/memoir/non-fiction piece completely written out. It can still be very rough, even written out in outline form, but you know the beginning, middle and end, or you have written out every scene you'd intended to write when you wrote the list out when you first had the book idea. This is a very exciting time but also a little dangerous, because the exhilaration can also lead to despair when you realize how much still needs to be done. So, *it's very important to celebrate here, and fix your next completion point.*

* The second completion point is when you've taken that first rough draft and modified it enough so that it is readable for someone else. Scenes and dialogue and description are now incorporated. This is where you are now. *Celebrate.*

* The third completion point is when you've added in all the things you forgot or didn't realize needed to be in, after you have reread the second version. And, you've

also put everything into the right place, and taken out what doesn't belong. We will be working on this in this chapter. *Celebrate.*

* The fourth completion point is when you carefully review the last manuscript and have finessed the words and sentences. This is probably what most people would think of as the complete manuscript. But here's what you haven't realized. Your "final draft" is the first draft to the agent or editor upon whose desk it lands next. (Whether you are going the traditional route or not, you should still have an editor review the manuscript). After its acceptance by an agent or publisher, it will require three more rounds. *Are you celebrating?*

* The fifth completion point is when you make the editing suggestions your agent or editor gives you. *Celebrate.*

* The sixth completion point is when you make the copy-editing suggestions when the book is in production at the publisher. *Celebrate.*

* The seventh completion point is when you make the final corrections to the page proofs you receive from the printer before it goes to press! *Big celebration!*

So you see, it's a long process. It is like a marathon, and you can look at each completion point as a mini-marathon. And this is why it is so important to acknowledge and celebrate each stage you do complete. You may even want to plan special events to celebrate: a dinner at your favorite restaurant, a massage, a book publication party. Do something now to acknowledge what you have done, before you move on to the editing described in this chapter.

Let's look at editing now. First, structural things. The first question is, What things do you know now that you've finished the draft that you didn't know in the beginning? An example of this might be, if you are writing a mystery novel, that you realized you needed to add a clue that you didn't have in the beginning, which requires adding a chapter or a scene. Or even, you thought one character was the murderer but it turned out to be another one. M. Night Shyamalan wrote the entire screenplay for *The Sixth Sense* before he realized the most important point—the main character was a ghost.

If you are writing nonfiction, you may have discovered information that you didn't know when you first started. Or, through working closely with the material, you've gained an insight that you didn't have at first. Another thing you may understand now that you didn't at first is what the actual point of the book is. I know it may seem ridiculous, but sometimes you have to write it all out to see what it is you are really trying to say. I love the story of the making of *Casablanca*. They were shooting the movie in order (a rarity) partly because the script wasn't finished. They literally didn't know the ending and were prepared to shoot two. In one, of course, Ingrid Bergman gets on the plane with her husband and leaves Humphrey Bogart. In the other, she stays. You never heard of that option because once they filmed the first one, they *knew* it was the ending. They had to actually create it ("write" it) to see what they had.

Take a minute and answer these questions here:

What do I know now about my manuscript that I didn't know when I started?

What is the real theme of the manuscript?

How do I want people to feel when they have finished the last page?

What changes do I need to make in the manuscript now?

If you have really changed or narrowed the focus, it could be helpful at this point to reread the manuscript, looking at each chapter or scene from this perspective. If it doesn't fit the new focus, it doesn't fit anymore. Don't throw it out though, you may have material here for another book. Create another file on your computer and cut and paste the material in there. In fact, just to free yourself, make sure to save the first version of the manuscript as Draft One (see Chapter 7 for details), and create a new file so that you will feel more comfortable cutting.

For instance, if you've decided that the focus of the book should be much narrower and you have too many plot points, knowing your theme and making the list of things you now know can help in deciding which things to lift out. Maybe you discovered your theme is about finding love and you've got too many scenes that are about self-discovery, which do not move the story forward. Or, you thought you were writing a biography but realized you actually only want to focus on the most relevant decision in the person's life, and you can let go of the part that describes where he was born and grew up. You could also decide that everything is staying, it just needs to be in a slightly different order.

It may help at this point to take a step back and look at the manuscript from a different perspective. I mean this quite literally. Many writers find it helpful to use some kind of visual outline to see how the plot flows or the context of the material being covered. When I began "throwing the structure up on the board," as I described in Chapter 3, "Seducing the Muse," I hadn't realized that this particular form of visualizing does not come naturally to everyone as it does to me. I always "see" the books I work on this way in my head, and that's probably why it's always been easy for me to edit manuscripts—I can see the whole all the time. Once I realized this was not natural for most people, I began teaching the method for visualizing it. I compare it to adding a long column of numbers. Some people can do it in their heads but it's really helpful to see it on the board.

When you are in the middle of writing, you are at the level of word, sentence, paragraph. You are in the forest and all you see are trees. When you use some form of visual to see the entire book at once, it's as if you are hopping in a helicopter and are hovering over the forest looking at its length and breadth. This gives you perspective. It helps you see the shape your work currently has, and you can usually quickly see what fits and what doesn't, what has to be moved, and where it needs to go. Or, it may not be so obvious, but you can quickly move the large pieces around and see whether they would fit better in a different pattern. It's like moving furniture around in your living room. The other thing that creating a visual can do for you is help you lighten up about your work, and play with it a bit. When you can hold it lightly, you can see more options more quickly.

There are many different ways to create a visual, and there is no one right way. Pick one that seems fun to you, or easy to do. Here are some ideas:

* Write an outline of each chapter and what it contains on a pad, being as brief as possible, then go back and do it even more succinctly.

* Get a roll of architecture paper (which is fun, and it's very long so you aren't in danger of running out, or fearful of ruining anything), and some different colored markers or pencils. Starting with the first chapter, write the brief highlights, using different colors for different themes, unrolling more paper for the next chapter until the entire contents of the book are on the page somewhere. Then cut it and hang it up.

* Print a tiny version. This method was used by a student in one of my classes. She found it in a book called *Novel Metamorphosis* by Darcy Pattison, a book on revising novels. It's an easy way to get to see the big picture, although I think it is more helpful for fiction than non-fiction. The instructions are simple. Take the chapter breaks out of the file. (Save a version first, of course, under a different name.) Single space it, and reduce the font until you have about thirty pages total. Then print it and spread it out on the floor. What you will see is the proportions of your different chapters, and

where the dialogue appears. You will probably end up using colored markers and post-its to mark what you see needs fixing. Another way to accomplish this is to look at the outline view or thumbnail view (using the navigation panel) under View in Microsoft Word. See Chapter 7 for more information on this.

* Use a large whiteboard or a giant pad of post-it paper, and at least four different colored markers. Pick a color for each storyline, or each theme, and plot them on the paper simultaneously. For instance, if it's a novel or memoir, the page might contain a timeline and you plot each different section, one beneath the next. (This is the method I described in Chapter 4.) I was helping one client struggling to complete her fourth nonfiction book by her deadline. I quickly saw that she was struggling because there were many complex pieces to the story she wanted to tell simply. I brought over my oversized post-its and began papering the wall in front of her desk, using markers to show her the historical timeline of events she was writing about with one color, and then we used another color to show the themes needing to be emphasized. It was only when we'd covered not just the wall but two walls of windows as well (it was a small office) that she began to understand that she couldn't tell everything and would have to let go of some pieces of history to tell the story she was focused on.

* Create a storyboard. Storyboarding is literally creating pictures for each scene. It is used in the film industry to plan shots, but writers can use it too to more clearly see the flow of the storyline.

* Move furniture. By this I mean, take some index cards and write a word or two that tells you what each scene is, and then just reorder them and see what it looks like a different way.

* A very simple way to get clarity on the structure is to write out the timeline of the book. You can do this on any pad but using the post-it or architecture paper can make it easier. You may find themes emerge as you write the events out on the line. You may also find it helpful to use an actual printed calendar if you are writing a novel. You can see days of the week, and mark what different characters are doing when.

Sometimes the process of putting all this information down can be helpful by itself. You become so busy with index cards or colors, you don't even realize it and a tidbit of information just emerges in your brain, or a solution to a thorny plot point emerges. You have found a way to successfully engage your subconscious by keeping your conscious self really busy! Remember to play with it. If you are not having luck one way, just stop and try another on the list.

Once you are done, it can be a revelation. You may suddenly see connections, or juxtapositions, that you'd missed when in the thick of it. Or, you may notice some glaring omissions. You may see patterns and themes you hadn't thought about—or those you realize you need to emphasize.

Here's what to do next

Once you are clear on what the focus of the book is (through one or more of these techniques) and how you want it to be ordered, you need to go back to the manuscript and begin making the changes. If you need to move a lot of things around, first make a copy of the current version so you aren't worried about losing anything. Then, just put everything where you want it to go. Mark places where you know you need to put in transitions. Mark where you know you will need to be adding new things. It can be helpful to make a separate list, with page references. This helps you see your progress as you make your way through the list. You may also find a color-coding system to work well here. Use different colored flags or post-its—one for transitions, and one for additions. If there are whole sections you know need to go, create a new file for them, called either "snippets" or "leftovers," or the title of your next book. This can make it easier to let go.

I had one client who was extremely visual, and happened to work in book design. When she decided she had to move things around in her manuscript, she found it helpful to change the color of the type itself so she knew where she had moved material from. I found it difficult to read all the different colored type, but it worked for her!

How to Let Go

What if you still don't want to cut the material? This is not at all unusual. After all, you've worked so hard on this book. You've poured your deepest self into it. And now it looks like huge chunks of it, or even tiny precious pieces of it, don't fit. What do you do when you don't want to let it go? This is hard for any writer. And I actually think the courage to cut is the thing that separates the pros from the amateurs when it comes to writing. (I am not speaking here of line editing—the sentences and words—which I discuss below. I mean chunks of material—scenes, concepts, paragraphs, pages.)

Ask yourself: Are you serving yourself? Or are you serving the book?

How can you tell? My answer is, serving yourself is about pride and ego; the book has different needs. When asked, "How do you know when you are done writing a play?" Wendy Wassertein responded, "When I've cut my best line."

By this time, your book has become something outside of you. It's being fully formed. One of the necessary stages in the process is that it not be part of *you* any longer. Just as in giving birth, your job is to hold onto it long enough for it to gestate, and survive on its own in the world. And then, let it go. There might be deeper issues than you realize at work here, if you are holding on to something when your clear-headed, detached editor-self can see that it doesn't belong. You might want to turn to Chapter 6, "How Do You Know When You Are Done?" to see if some of the material on perfectionism fits you. You may be holding on because you don't want to be done yet, or for other reasons. But, let's say that's not the case for you. You just don't want to cut this. There are two possibilities.

One, it needs to be cut and you don't want to let it go.
Two, it doesn't need to be cut and you just think it does.

How do you know which it is? My guess is, if you think it doesn't fit, it probably doesn't. And again I say, think of the needs of the book and not your own. To make the best possible book, does it need to go? If the answer is yes, then you don't need me to tell you what you need to do. And I've already suggested several times that the most helpful thing in these cases is to realize that it doesn't necessarily mean that what you throw out will never be used; it may end up in another book down the line. That's why I suggest creating a separate file for all the things you cut, or even several files with their own names so you know what you have.

Let's say it's actually the second situation—you just *think* it needs to be cut. Why would that be true? Why would you be thinking of cutting something that should stay? Overzealousness, a fear that the manuscript is too long and something has to go. There's one other action you can take to help discern the truth, and it's one I'm loath to tell you, because I've seen it backfire for many people. That is, ask someone you trust to read the manuscript for you and give you their opinion. I am afraid to suggest it because it is very likely you will pick someone you think is safe and trustworthy, who may actually have an unhealed inner critic who may come out and bite you, or worse, set back your writing by a week, a month, or even a year. (I have seen instances of this.) I've created a list to help you.

Tips on how to select a good and appropriate reader

* Pick someone you trust, but not necessarily someone you know well. Sometimes a comparative stranger can be more helpful than a close friend.

* Pick someone who regularly reads the kind of book you've written (i.e. memoir, chick lit, mystery, history, etc.)

* Pick someone who actively engages their own creativity. It doesn't have to be a fellow writer, it could be a musician or even a scientist, but if they use their own creativity, they are less likely to have an unhealed inner critic.

* If you do pick a fellow writer, see if you can exchange writing so that you are on an equal footing.

It's probably a bad idea to pick:

* Your spouse
* Your sibling who has always been jealous of you
* Your mother who wishes you were a doctor
* A writer who has never finished a manuscript

Another way to approach this is just to proceed as if it doesn't need to be fixed, follow through with all the rest of the suggestions in this book, and begin sending it out to agents or editors. If you begin to receive the same feedback from people, perhaps you know that, indeed, it did need to come out.

Of course, the reverse can be true. I have occasionally been asked to edit something and given feedback that something was missing, only to discover that the author had written that very thing, but taken it out.

I had one client who received feedback from more than one reader that she needed to cut her story down. She did so. Then when she was receiving similar comments from agents, she turned to a professional line editor, whose comments came back requesting some of the very material she had cut! So she put it back in.

Your Inner Guide

The real issue underneath all this is we want to get to the point of discernment, and trust that discernment. You want to avoid two pitfalls: trying to please your reader at the expense of the writing; and being afraid of letting the real truth of your writing out. Ultimately, you need to have faith in your own inner guide, your inner creative self. I trust that part of you. It is there, as long as you can reach it clearly, and without all the landmines and dragons that we all create for ourselves on the path of creativity.

How can you begin to trust this inner guide, your inner editor, more? I think the only thing that really works is reading good books. Keep good company for yourself. Good writing always inspires us to be our best, and it is our best teacher. It's like the way a good tennis player will always want to play with someone better, to stay sharp and to learn more. When students ask me how to recognize good books, I tell them first to trust that books they like and want to read again, are good. They may not be classic literature, but they must have something compelling. Many books now considered classics were thought to be "trashy" when first published (like Raymond Chandler). Others were written in such a different style, ushering in a new form, that they weren't recognized as great immediately—many because they were also from subcultures not recognized by the mainstream.

But if you really want a primer in good writing, going back to the classics is easy. If you aren't sure, or are intimidated, ask a librarian. Or look at the lists provided for students to read over the summer. Nothing wrong either with reading good children's literature.

When reading, re-read. I usually read a book fast the first time, because I'm caught up in the plot and want to know what happens. I read it a second time to appreciate the writing. When you have begun to line edit your own book you will see that you can't help but notice when an author writes an elegant sentence, and appreciate compact description or good dialogue. In *How to Read a Book*, Mortimer Adler (of Great Books fame) recommends reading a book three times.

Transitions

Once you have completed the cutting, you can go back and create the links or transitions from one chapter to the next.

Whether this is fiction or nonfiction, the process is actually the same. I always find that before I begin, I think it will be hugely complicated and difficult to get from where I left off in one chapter to the revised or new or totally relocated following chapter. But when I actually get into the text, it turns out a simple obvious sentence will work (usually for nonfiction), or that there's some very simple texture (I think of it as connecting tissue) that will put the pieces together for a novel. If you are struggling try the following:

What is the point you are stopping at in the first chapter or section?

Where are you starting the next chapter?

What changes from the first to the second chapter?

What are the points of connection between the two?

Can you pick one of those points and use it as the link?

Can you write one or two sentences that would take you from the end of the first chapter to the start of the second?

If you are jumping in time, do you actually need a transition? Or can you simply cut to the new section, and weave in a bit of background in the second or third paragraph?

Line Editing

Now we come to the next phase of the editing process, the writing itself. There are probably a bunch of things you know need fixing. This is where the old-fashioned editing style can come in handy. After you have made the main structural changes, I would print out a hard copy of the book—double-spaced!—and work from that, with a pen, to make the revisions. (I know no one wants to waste paper, but at a certain point it would be like trying to build a house without nails—these are the tools of your trade and you need to give yourself permission to use them.) This part is laborious and can even be painstaking, but it is well worth it to create a clean manuscript. You may want to give yourself permission to read it through once and just mark what you notice (I'd mark it right in the manuscript, and also keep a list of where changes need to be made so you can find it quickly), and then go back chapter by chapter in a more thorough way.

You may find yourself inspired as you are reading to add the new material you see is needed. Most likely these will be small pieces, sentences and transitional paragraphs. If it's a small thing, and you can write it and then turn back to reading, by all means do so. Keep in mind, though, that any new material requires writing in flow again. That is very different from the mindset required for editing. Don't expect to be able to flip easily back and forth between the two mindsets as you go. You will probably either get stuck and find yourself unable to write in flow, or flowing easily and completely losing track of the editing. So, whether you go through all of the manuscript doing the line editing and making notes to go back, or you edit in the morning and write new scenes in the afternoon; the point is not to expect yourself to be able to flip the switch and go from one to the other in an instant.

I once watched a fiction writer let go of good sentences, words, images, just because they were not needed. They cluttered, but didn't enhance, the writing. I believe this is what William Faulkner refers to in his famous quote to "Kill your darlings." I'm continually awed by the courage that's required to get up every day and serve the book, not yourself, continually cutting, not adding, until you get down to the core and finally can let it go, because nothing remains but the essence. It's like Michalangelo cutting away what didn't belong from the marble, until what he left us with was the David.

Martha Albrand, quoted in *20th Century Crime & Mystery*, writes, "All writing is a process of elimination.'"

There are many good books with tips on how to be your

own line editor (see Appendix for suggestions). Pick one you like and follow its guidelines if you feel you need help here. I will give you one caution: be sure not to decimate your own style in favor of someone else's idea of what "right" is. There are many ways to put sentences together. There are even instances where incorrect grammar is okay. And sometimes there's more to it than just grammar. I once had a student come to me puzzled by some editing feedback she'd gotten from a friend. As we reviewed it together, I realized why she and her friend had such different ideas about the material. My student wrote in an auditory style, and her friend was more visual. The friend thought she should write the same way, and that that was the "correct" way, and the way publishers preferred.

These patterns of thinking, speaking, and writing, are laid out in Neurolinguistic Programming (NLP). The theory is that our brains process information through one of our five senses. Although there are some people who mainly use the sense of taste or smell (often they are professional chefs or perfumers) most people are either more visual, auditory, or kinesthetic. And for these purposes, kinesthetic can be either physical or emotional feeling. Most likely, when you write, you are either picturing scenes and writing them down, picturing words or structure and writing it down, hearing words and writing them down, or feeling things at a very deep level and writing them down.

We seem to have been moving as a population from being mostly auditory in the Nineteenth century to being mostly visual in the Twenty-first (kinesthetic has been in the minority in both). Think of how Dickens or Austen was experienced in the 1800's—read aloud in the living room. Think of how we experience novels today—reading them alone, looking at the pages. And often later watching them as movies or television shows.

Here are some examples. This is the opening of Dickens' *A Tale of Two Cities* (1859):

"It was the best of times, it was the worst of times,
it was the age of wisdom, it was the age of foolishness,
it was the epoch of belief, it was the epoch of incredulity,
It was the season of Light, it was the season of Darkness,
it was the spring of hope, it was the winter of despair,
we had everything before us, we had nothing before us,
we were all going direct to Heaven, we were all going direct the other way..."

Clearly this was meant to be read aloud. It's almost like poetry. This is the opening line of Austen's *Pride and Prejudice* (1813):

"It is a truth universally acknowledged that a young man of good fortune must be in want of a wife."

Both of these books take a few pages to land us with one character and begin the story.

This is the start of *Cold Mountain* by Charles Frazier (1997):

"At the first gestures of morning, flies began stirring. Inman's eyes and the long wound at his neck drew them, and the sound of their wings and the touch of their feet were soon more potent than a yardful of roosters in rousing a man to wake. So he came to yet one more day in the hospital ward. He flapped the flies away with his hands and looked across the foot of his bed to an open triple-hung window."

And here is classic Danielle Steel, *The Promise* (1989):

"The early morning sun streamed across their backs as they unhooked their bicycles in front of Eliot House on the Harvard campus. They stopped for a moment to smile at each other. It was May and they were very young. Her short hair shone in the sunshine, and her eyes found his as she began to laugh."

You will notice that Frazier combined sound and feeling, and this will certainly hold up when read aloud, yet we have a visual sense of the scene by the fourth sentence. Danielle Steel is all visual, as is a lot of commercial fiction.

It seems to me that there is a lot of pressure on writers today to be more visual. All the "how to write" books advise it, and it certainly makes it easier to transfer them to film or television. And yet, I still feel there's an important place for a strong auditory narrative—one that sounds great when read aloud (or in your head). Auditory writers hear the words, and want a certain pace and flow that they hate to interrupt to get to a scene faster, or even to be grammatically correct. (Often they need to write quickly to get down the words they are hearing.)

I think the best approach is to be conscious of your own bent, to consider enhancing your writing by using other senses, and to be true to yourself. Certainly even the most visual writer needs to have good dialogue, which is auditory, and every piece of writing is enhanced when the scene is set clearly, as visual writers tend to do easily.

You can use different techniques to get unstuck depending on which type you are. If you are visual, you may want to play with some images. Take a break from writing and make a collage, see if that evokes anything. Or make a chart and see if you can move things around. If you are auditory, imagine talking the issue over with someone. Write down what you say. Let your characters talk to you. And if you are kinesthetic, you may want to get up and pace while you are writing. Or print things out and move them around on your desk. Or write longhand for awhile. Be aware that unlike the other types, you may need to think the writing all the way through before you write it down. It is a slower process but it works too.

Whatever your natural preference, there are certain basics that will improve anyone's writing. Clarity is good. I love how true it is that if you are unclear anywhere, it shows up as murky writing. Use this time, then, to be very clear on what you are saying. You may find it helpful to look over the material in Chapter 2, "Finding Your Voice," particularly the exercise "who are you, and why are you writing this book?"

One thing that should be painfully obvious to you by now is that every writer has their "writing thing" – the mistake that is made over and over in the writing. It could be one word that you use over and over (like "over and over.") It could be that you tend to frame sentences so they are passive, not active. It could be that you overuse adverbs. Whatever it is, forgive yourself for doing it over and over in your first draft. We all do. Just correct it now.

Then enter the changes into the manuscript, and print it out again for a final read-through. You can call this your second draft. Now you are ready to send it out!

Commitment:

Even though you are up to the editing phase of your writing, it's important to keep committing each week. If you find it more helpful now, you can think in terms of a time commitment rather than a page commitment (that is, one hour not three pages) since the work you are doing does not always correlate with page length.

Also do keep in mind that once you have switched from flow to editing mode, the pace of your progress will feel very different. At times it may feel like you are hardly making any. Being consistent here makes all the difference. I often tell students this is when you want to look down at your feet and just keep walking, rather than looking up to the top of the mountain where you are headed.

Another tip is to see if there's some way you can engage your flow writing. Do you have a short piece you can work on a little? Some ideas for the next book? Balancing your time between flow and editing can help you with both. Remember how Jane Austen always worked on her new novel in the morning, and edited her completed novel in the afternoon.

How many times can you show up to write this week? _____

How long can you write each time? ________________

And what do you want to work on when you first sit down?

____

____

Chapter 6 

How Do You Know When You Are Done?

How do you know when you are done?

How do you know that you have finished your edits, and the manuscript is ready to send out?

How can you be sure it's ready?

Here is a checklist:

* Have you read the entire book through?
* When you read it through, did you take notes of things you thought were problematic?
* Did you address all those things?
* Have you read it through with a pen, making the changes needed to clean up the writing?
* Do you know what your "writing thing" is and have you searched for it and weeded it out?
* Have you used your outline from the structure exercise, and is everything included?

If you have answered yes to all these, then it is highly likely that you are done. If you are still not satisfied, let's look deeper.

It can be very easy to get hung up in perfectionism. Remember the *Sufferings of Young Werther* story from Chapter 1? Perfection is actually the enemy here. It CANNOT be perfect, at least not on this plane of existence. You must let that go. If you modify your goal, and shoot for it to be as good as you can make it…well, even here you are asking for trouble. Let's make the goal be that you have double-checked all your work and you've included everything you meant to say here. Now you are going to move on.

What you are balancing is a sincere desire to do a good and thorough job, with a tortured perfectionism that is actually a cover for your intense fear of what might happen when you are actually done. This brings us back to what I started with: starting and finishing are the two most difficult parts of writing, and fear of starting is fear of failure, and fear of finishing is fear of success.

When you are this far along, and this close to done, you are beginning to believe you might actually do this, you might actually finish this and it might be published. So any fears that you have about what that might lead to will begin popping up. But your psyche is subtle, so it pops up in disguise, and its disguise is this voice that says, you can do better. It is really the voice of your critic wanting to protect you from what it thinks will happen when this work is exposed to the world, but it's pretending to be your detached, healthy editing-self. I will talk more about how to deal head-on with these fears, but first, let's investigate how you can tell whether this voice is the critic or your editing self.

How can you recognize which voice it is?

Danger signs of the Critic:

* You keep thinking you need to edit more, but you realize you are starting to change things back to how they were when you started.
* You keep thinking you need a huge block of time to do some more research.
* You think it really makes sense to ditch everything you have and start over.
* You doubt decisions you already made about what stays and what goes, or what order to put things in.
* You find yourself saying things like "It's all crap," or "I'll never finish."

Take a moment here and jot down what you think you still have to do for your manuscript to be complete:

Now, review the list. If your best friend were saying these things about her manuscript, would you think it was the truth, or ridiculous? Is it the voice of your healthy editor or your inner critic, or a mix of both? Take a moment to circle the ones you think are valid, and cross out the steps that you recognize as the critic.

Remember that the critic is only trying to protect you from criticism from the outer world. We will be looking at healthier ways to protect yourself than never finishing anything that can be criticized.

Most often, at this stage, when writers think they aren't done it is the Inner Critic. However, there are times when writers have had ideas at this juncture that not only were valid, they greatly improved the book. This is why I think it so important to discern what the truth is here.

I had one client who'd been working on a nonfiction book for awhile, and I thought it was good, and very close to done. But he began resisting finishing. I pressed, he didn't give in, so I backed off. I thought he was just afraid to finish. Much to my surprise, a few weeks later, he came up with an entirely fresh perspective on the material. It changed everything, and made it much better. Had I succeeded in my persuasions, a book would have been published, but it wouldn't have been as good.

Another time, I'd worked with a writer on a novel. Again, I thought it was good. Really good. I didn't want her to change anything. I wanted her to start sending it to agents. But she resisted. She wasn't satisfied. This time I let go more quickly. And she ended up rewriting the book on a much higher plane, that I'd had no idea was there.

This is why I have a huge respect for the creative process. Sometimes your inner creative self really does know something, and really does want to make the material better. And it shouldn't be forced to settle. Struggle is actually an important part of the creative process, and it can be necessary to wrestle in the unknown for awhile.

So, again, how can you tell the difference between the two?

The real thing to focus on is how it makes you feel. If you feel a horrible feeling in the pit of your stomach like you are fundamentally no good, it's the critic. If you are intensely afraid of someone else picking it apart when they read it after you are done, it's the critic. If you feel a motivation to do something to fix the writing or add a piece or even the need to go very deep and get very still and reflect, then it's probably discernment.

Remember, creativity is motivating, the critic is deadening or paralyzing. It is the critic causing your procrastinating out of fear.

I promised you I'd talk more about how to face the fears you have head on. Here is the easy way to approach it. Make a fears list. Right now, without thinking too much, write out ten fears you have about the book being done:

1.
2.
3.
4.
5.
6.
7.
8.
9.
10.

Just before I finished my first book (*It's About Time: Finding Magic, Power and Ease in Your Life*), I was teaching a writing class and only one person showed up. Since she was having similar issues to me, we decided to use the class time to work on it. We each did a fear list. Then, when I saw how different from one another my items were, I put them onto a timeline of things that related to the book before it was published, and things having to do with afterwards.

Go ahead and mark yours on here.

I immediately saw that most of the items on my list (there were about ten) had to do with things after publication (things like, How do I market the book? And, What if no one comes to my book signing?—incidentally I had over 100 people there). I decided that for the time being, I didn't even have to look at those. There would be time later to deal with them one at a time. There were only four items that pertained to the manuscript. And when I boiled them down, there were two issues. One was very specific. I was really afraid to send the manuscript off to the production department because I was not sure if I had left something important out. I decided all I needed to do to assuage that fear was to set aside time (four hours, in this case) and sit down and read the manuscript through once more. I did that, and then became willing to send it on. I say this in this much detail because until I actually wrote my fears down, I was paralyzed and unwilling to move forward. But once I was conscious and clear about the fears, I was able to take action. And then move on.

Look at your list and divide it the same way. See if there are some simple actions you can take that will dispel your fears.

The other issue was more fundamental. It was the fear that I find is underneath most of the procrastination people have when they are close to done. It is simply this: What if people don't like me anymore? Or, What if I am no longer a part of my group?

This is not a small fear, and it turns out not to be as silly as it may sound. In order to survive as a species, humans have had to rely on the group, so we literally have it bred in our bones to fit in and get along. Finishing your book, having it published, maybe even having it sell well—that could be challenging to some groups you are in. Maybe you are in a writing group and no one else has been able to get as far as you. Maybe your family doesn't approve. This is not easy. Because it may in fact be true that you will lose some relationships if you achieve this goal. But I hope you will be able to see that it will also qualify you for a new group: the group of people who have completed their books.

What makes this issue harder is that you are probably being triggered about something that happened in your childhood, some time when you were ostracized or threatened with it, if you did something you loved. A student who was feeling this very deeply told me the question that helped her the most with this was: What is different now than when you were young? In other words, how are you better equipped today to handle it?

The truth is, when we are on this journey of creativity, of writing, we do have to let go of a lot. The thing is, in the end, it's worth it.

But also remember about the "Blocks are only there in case you want to stop" exercise in Chapter 3, "Seducing the Muse." If you feel you are not ready, you don't have to keep going. You can stop here. You can put the manuscript in a drawer until you do feel ready. Or even leave instructions for its publication after you die. But do it consciously. Don't keep struggling with it.

A special note to those of you writing memoirs or fiction that is based on real-life incidents. You may have a very particular reason to be fearful of publication. You may not want to hurt people who are part of your story. Or, you may fear what people will do if you tell the truth about them. I would ask you to apply the same reasoning to your list. Is there anything you can do to assuage the fear? Can you publish the book anonymously? If it is safe, can you approach the people who are in the story and gauge their feeling about it? If you have any concerns about your safety or those of others that you believe are legitimate and you can't resolve, then the safest place for this story right now may well be in a drawer. I want to give you permission to do what you need to do to take care of yourself. You can't force yourself to be ready. When you are, you are. But being able to acknowledge it, and make your decision from a conscious place, is much more empowering than continuing to do research, or editing the same piece over and over.

Here's another story for you. One of my favorite books is *Gifts Differing* by Isabel Briggs Myers. She was a perfectionist (actually if you read the book or know the Myers-Briggs type indicator, she was an INFP, one acronym for it is I Never Find Perfection!). She worked on this book, literally her magnum opus and her life's work, for almost her entire professional life (along with developing the MBTI Instrument). She kept reworking it, thinking it could be better. Finally, when she was literally on her death bed at 75, her son took it from her and finished it. Meanwhile, had she been willing to let it go sooner, it could have been helping many people (it is a classic work).

Early in his career, Picasso gave a framed painting to some friends. Twenty years later, they returned to him with it, now a priceless masterpiece. The frame had broken and they wanted him to repair it. He took the frame off, put the canvas on his easel, and began painting again! To their minds, he was ruining their masterpiece. He saw where he could improve on the earlier draft. What is the point of this story? That nothing is ever actually done. You just decide to stop working on it.

There's another issue that can come up for some people, especially if it's a novel you've been working on. That is, you might miss it. You may have come to love your characters, and you've enjoyed spending time with them. Just as you feel disappointment when you come to the end of a good novel, you may not want this to be over. There's actually only one solution to this. Let go so that another story and more characters can come to you. Either that, or do a sequel or prequel with the same characters! Or, go investigate some characters who were peripheral to this story. (See Chapter 9, "What's Next?" for help with this.)

In a similar way, people working on memoirs may also have trouble being done. I have had several people who were writing about family members who had died. "If I'm done," they tell me, "then she/he will really be gone."

Here's where you have to be like a good parent with a child. Is it kind to the child to keep it at home with you always, to never let it grow up and move out to have its own life? No. What you do is, you give the child everything you can while they are young, the tools they need and the information they can use, and then you trust that they can take all that with them when they leave. In this case, you've done the best job you can with the manuscript, you've given it your all, and you need to let go now so that others get to experience it.

There's another thing that may happen to you as you are completing that last edit of the manuscript. You may become sick of it. This is actually a good thing (as long as you don't throw it away!). You are like the woman who is nine months and two weeks pregnant. You can't wait to have it be done already! You are ready for the next stage. This is actually appropriate. This is the end of the creative cycle with this book (i.e. this pregnancy), and you are ready to move on. I hope you will be moving on to begin a new cycle with another creative project. Turn to Chapter 9 for some tips on where to begin. Chapter 7 is more practical, with information on how to get the manuscript ready for publication. Chapter 8 is an overview of the publishing process.

I always end my classes with my favorite exercise. The point of it is to help you move beyond where you might be stuck. I hope you like it too.

This is a guided visualization, so first make sure you can take at least five or ten minutes undisturbed, and find a comfortable place to sit with your feet flat on the floor. You may wish to read the exercise over first, or even record it to play it back to yourself.

Now take a deep breath in and relax as you exhale. Take another deep breath in and as you exhale feel your shoulders drop. Allow your body to sink into the chair, feel the floor holding your feet up.

Imagine that you are standing in your living room. Whatever it is that had to be done to complete your book has been done. Whatever had to happen to connect you to the right editor and publisher, has happened. And today you are waiting for a copy of your book to arrive.

The doorbell rings. You open the door and there is the U.P.S. person with a brown package for you. You say thank you, then close the door. You rip open the package, and there in your hands is your completed book.

Take a moment to breathe, and notice how you feel in your body. Feel the weight of the book in your hands. Look at the front cover, the spine, the back cover. You can even lift the book up and smell it. Then, open the book.

Notice the feel of the pages. Look at the copyright page. Turn to the table of contents. Notice the running heads at the top or bottom of the page. Notice the typeface. Are there pictures or drawings? Charts? Take your time flipping through the book. Look at the back and see if there's a picture of you. Are there endorsements from others? Again, take a breath and notice how you feel in your body. Take your time exploring your book.

When you are ready, take the book and bring it to the special place you've already prepared somewhere in your home. It could be on your coffee table. It could be on the shelf with all your favorite authors. You may have set up a special lighted bookshelf just for this. Whatever it is, take your book and place it there.

Take a step back and look at it. Notice how you feel. Then, pick up your phone and imagine calling the first person you have to call to say, "My book is done! My book is done!"

When you are ready, slowly bring yourself back into the room. Take a deep breath. Wiggle your toes. Then take a pad and paper and jot down any notes of what you want to remember.

For many of my students, this exercise is a profound experience. Until they allowed themselves to imagine it, they hadn't realized how much they'd longed for this moment, and how far away they thought it was. Often there are tears. But also, there is inspiration. Many get ideas they hadn't thought of before. And many just have a renewed confidence that this will happen.

Feel free to revisit this exercise as often as you like!

Commitment:

Take the list you created of what remains to be done (the legitimate reasons not the critic's complaints!), and commit to taking action on it in your time this week.

Because the tasks are so left-brained, you may also want to see if there's a way to engage your flow. Can you begin working on a new idea with some of your time this week, while still committing to completing this draft?

How many times can you show up to write this week? _____

How long can you write each time? ________________

And what do you want to work on when you first sit down?

____

____

Chapter 7

Formatting Basics

I've included this chapter here (and not, say, as Chapter 1) because while it can actually be helpful from the minute you begin writing, if you start with it you will definitely put yourself into editing mode, and out of flow. But when you are ready, these tips and techniques can really help you in the writing itself. Most will apply to whatever program you use for writing, but some are specific to Microsoft Word, since that is the program most writers use.

Note: I originally began writing this chapter, and then realized how many details there actually are. So I include the basics here, and then created an ebook, *Microsoft Word for Writers*, which goes into greater specific detail. If you are looking for step by step instruction in Word, that is where to look.

Managing Documents

When you first began to write your book, you probably just opened a new file in Word and started typing. You didn't think about how to organize it, you were probably just grateful you got started. But now maybe you have 100 pages and you aren't sure what you've got and you've been having trouble finding paragraphs you know you already wrote. This is where it's handy to know a few tricks about managing large documents. It helps to start using some of these tricks from the very beginning but it's never too late to go back and get started.

Naming

The name you choose for the file is very important. I always call my first file whatever the title of the manuscript is with the word "draft" after it, which to me means it's my initial raw writing. Then, when I edit the file, I always use "save as" (in the file menu on Word) and change the name to the title and the number 1 after it instead of "draft." So this manuscript's first file name was "Complete That Book Draft." (When you use "save as," you create a copy of the file under a new name and then have two versions.) I change the number for each edited version. This way I always have the original saved if I accidentally make too many edited changes and want to go back to the way it was. Of course, once named, it is crucial to keep working only on the most recent file. That's also why I always keep the initial file name the same. When I arrange my files alphabetically, I can see all the different versions and I know which is most recent.

I also always create a separate folder for each manuscript so I don't have anything else cluttering it up. I name it the working title of the project. It also allows me to see all my files for this manuscript at a glance, almost like a Table of Contents.

Dividing Into Chapters

The next question is how big you let your file get. In the beginning, you may want to use only one file because it's easier to do a search within only one document, plus it's small enough initially that you can scroll to the bottom easily. But here are some reasons to break your document into chapters or sections:

* If you begin dividing by chapter or section, it's easier to print only what you want and search and find within the chapter
* It's easier to keep track of the different edited versions. (Some chapters will require more editing than others.)
* It will help you stop rereading the entire book each time you open the file to write or edit.

Moving Through Your Document

As your document gets bigger (even if you have separated it into chapters), scrolling through becomes a pain, especially if you are trying to get to a specific place. So here are some tips for how to do this.

1. Use the scroll bar on the right to scroll down or up very quickly. You can also use the arrows at the base of the file (the single arrow for continuous scroll, the double arrow for page scroll).
2. Use the keyboard to page down (depending on your keyboard there are page arrow keys).
3. To get to a specific page, select the Edit menu from the menu bar, select "Go to" (the shortcut is "Command" or "Propeller" G on the keyboard) In the go to what box, page number should be highlighted. Simply type in the page number and hit enter. The page number you selected will appear.
4. To find a specific word or group of words, select "find"

from the edit menu. (Or hit "Command" or "Propeller" F on your keyboard). Type in the word you are looking for (it's handy to use an unusual word or a group of words you know does not appear frequently). Click on "find next" or hit enter on your keyboard. You will be taken to the first appearance of that word in the document. If it is not the correct word, hit enter again and it will take you to the next appearance. If you are having no luck, the word might be misspelled in either the document or the find box. This is why phrases can be handy.

5. A handy way to find your place in a manuscript if you know you need to be going back to something (let's say you aren't sure how you ultimately want to say something, or you know you need to write in more detail or look something up) is to use brackets right in the text. [Like this.] Then when you need to go back you simply do a find for a bracket. Even if you have several in the manuscript, it still doesn't take long to find the right one.

File back up

I hope I don't need to convince you why this is important, but I have a few stories for you about why you do want to back up your files frequently. First: an author whose work I'd published lived in the Oakland Hills. During the Oakland Hills fire in 1991, the fire stopped two houses away from her. Of course, she had no way of knowing this, so when the firefighters told her and all her neighbors to clear out, she had a half hour to gather important possessions. She took her photos, and her computer disks. (This was back in the days when files were stored on disks, remember?) Luckily, she always backed up, so she knew she had all her writing for her book right there. The second story is about me, and also ends happily, although it wasn't apparent for a while. I was in the process of transferring all my files from my old computer to my new computer several years ago, when the old computer died. That's right, in the process of backing up, the whole disk shut down. I had a lot of what I needed, but I was missing about half of the manuscript I was working on! I talked to a data retrieval company but I didn't want to spend the $2,000 it would cost to have them rescue my data. I had notes, and some of the material in hard copy. I kept writing new material and didn't worry too much about what I'd lost. I knew I could rewrite it. A year later, I found a computer guy who was able to get everything back - for only $200.

One more story. One of my clients accidently moved the file with all her writing into the trash, and then emptied the trash! So you see, losses can come in many ways for all different reasons. The simplest way to protect yourself is to consistently back up your work.

Here's What You Do:

There's more than one way to back up. These days, you can even pay money to have it done for you automatically. A company scans your hard drive and uploads it to their servers every day—now it's called a "cloud." For Mac users, there's iCloud for about $100 a year. A company called Mozy does it for $90 a year for Mac or PC. These are good, but remember there is still a delay between back-ups so it would be good to have at least one other method. But, simpler systems work fine. The important thing is to pick a method that works *for you* and do it *now*.

Here Are a Few Ideas:

* *Email yourself (and then don't open the email—it lives in the ethers. You can create a separate email account just for this.)*

Advantages: simple, you can access your file from any computer with the Internet, not affected by local natural disasters.

Disadvantages: relying on the email company to keep the email. Most don't guarantee that they won't lose your email. Still, this is better than nothing.

* *Back up from one computer to another*

Advantages: could be simple if you use more than one computer.

Disadvantages: if both computers are in the same place you could lose both in a natural disaster.

* *Use a thumb or flash drive (a small external hard drive that uses the USB port)*

Advantages: simple, and portable so you can carry it with you. Many writers I work with feel safer when they always have the latest version of their manuscript *with* them.

Disadvantages: it's not designed to be permanent storage, which means it can become corrupted or damaged (this happened to one of my students).

* *Use an external hard drive*

Advantages: very reliable, easy once it's set up, almost unlimited storage.

Disadvantages: If it's right next to your computer, you could lose both in a natural disaster.

* *Use CDs*

Advantages: cheap; fairly easy once you get used to it. If you mail it to someone else you will have it if an Act of God occurs.

Disadvantages: can't store as much on one, so you may need many.

✳ *Make a printout*

Advantages: it's nice to have a printout (a hard copy, on paper) regardless, and it's fairly easy to store.

Disadvantages: can't do it frequently, could still lose it, if it's in the same place as the computer.

You may want to use more than one way.

My Recommendation:

Pick two ways that are easy for you to do. One should happen every time you write; one should be monthly and put into a different location. So for instance, you can email yourself a new version monthly, and put the latest changes on your thumb drive. Or email yourself every time you write, and mail your mother a CD every month. Or put a CD in a safety deposit box. Keep in mind my examples: you want to protect against the most likely occurrence, a computer crash, but also prepare for the unlikely occurrence of an Act of God like a fire or earthquake.

If you have paid to use a "cloud," remember that it is still possible to lose writing in the time set between back-ups. I would still pick one other way to back up, each time you write.

Email and thumb drive are probably the easiest and cheapest, so…

Here's How to Do It:

Email:

1. Save the latest version of your file.
2. Open your email program and open a new email.
3. Address the email to yourself (you can even create a special

email account for this. See #7 below. You can also set it up on your email account server, see #8 below).

4. Click to attach your file and follow prompts to select the one you just saved.
5. Hit "Send."
6. When the email hits your inbox, don't open it. It will live in the ethers and you can claim it again from any computer with Internet access.
7. It may be convenient to create a separate email account for this. It's fairly simple to create a Gmail account that is free. You want to be sure not to download the email to your computer (which is what happens when you open it) because it could be erased automatically from your inbox.
8. If you log on to your email through a browser (That is, go to comcast.net or another Internet site like (gmail.com) and then sign onto your email account from there), you can create a folder on their server where big files and important files can be stored and won't get downloaded when you open your email locally. Follow your email account provider's instructions.

Thumb or Flash drive:

A thumb drive is a mini, external hard drive. You plug it in to the USB port on your computer, and it shows up as an icon on your screen. On the Mac, the icon will look like another hard drive. Simply drag and drop the latest version of your file into it, drag the thumb-drive icon into the Trash, remove the thumb drive from your computer, and you are done. Be careful to follow the protocol for removal, which usually means dragging the icon into the Trash before pulling the thumb drive out of the USB port. If you don't, you could lose or damage the files on the thumb drive. Also, you have to close any open files from the thumb drive before you can remove it. The rules are almost the same for the PC. You first have to locate the thumb drive icon, which should appear in the task bar along the bottom of your screen. Put your mouse over it and right-click. It will give you the option of "Remove External Drive Safely." Click on that option. It will tell you when it's safe to remove the thumb drive. It won't let you remove the drive if there are any files open, so make sure you close them all before you try to remove the drive.

Pagination and running heads

There's more than one way to paginate in Word. The best way, and the only way I would suggest using, is with running heads (called "header" or "footer" in Word). Here's why. It works better when you are managing large documents or combining documents. And it will also help you keep track of versions in your printouts. And finally, when it comes time for your manuscript to be sent off to an agent or editor, it will prevent your manuscript from getting mixed up with someone else's manuscript if it happens to fall off a shelf.

Here's how to do it:

1. Under "View" in the menu bar, select "header or footer"

You should be taken first to the header above the page you are in. It will look like a box, and you will see the words "header" and "close" in little buttons on the left . Don't click on "header," it will take you to the Elements Gallery which does very fancy things you don't need for a manuscript. Instead, insert your cursor into the box. Then, go to "View" again and select formatting palette. It's a floating box with many symbols and options. You can move it around your screen as needed so as not to interfere with your open document. Because you have selected "Header and Footer" you should see the tab for "Header and Footer" opened. Before going there, open the tab called "Alignment and Spacing" by clicking on the arrow. Select "align right." It looks like lines aligned with the margin on the right. Now your cursor should be at the right hand side of your page. Now, look under the tab for "Header and Footer" and select the page number sign: #. When you click it, the page number will automatically appear on the right hand side of your page, and it will fill in correctly on all the pages throughout the document. Put your cursor to the LEFT of the number and type the word "page." This makes it look nice on the header of your manuscript. Now, here's where it gets fun. I suggest next inserting the date by clicking on the date icon (the picture of the calendar), which means that every time you print the document that day's date will appear on the running head of all the pages, so you will know when you printed it. Then, and this is to be prepared for submission to agents, type in your last name, and the title of the book. If you don't yet know the title, use the word "untitled" for now. So your heading should now look like this:

Keenan, *Untitled Manuscrip*t, March 20, 2014 page 1

If you would rather have the page number at the bottom, you can use the same process for the footer. To get to the footer, scroll down to the bottom of the page where you will see a box that looks just like the box for the header. Insert your cursor and then follow the same instructions as for the header.

When you are done, just click the "close" button. From "Print Layout" view, you will still be able to see the header or footer, although you can't access it unless you go back in and select it. It won't be visible in "Draft" view, but will still print out.

Using Word to Edit Your Writing

Let's say you wrote a draft of a chapter, and then you rewrote it. You aren't sure if you like all of your revisions, but you want to review them all. This is where "Compare Documents" is helpful. I actually bought this software at MacWorld when it first came out, before Microsoft bought it and incorporated it into Word. It is a great tool, although it does have some limitations.

What it does is compare the two documents you choose, and mark up the manuscript (they call it "redlining") so that you can see what was changed from the first to the second version. Depending on whether you use a Mac or a PC, and which version of Word you are using, it also may tell you in the margin exactly what each change is.

Here's how to use it:

1. Go to "Tools" in the menu bar, and select "Track Changes" and then "Compare Documents"

2. A box will appear asking you which document you want to compare to "this" document (which means the document you have open). Be very careful to first open the *original* document, otherwise the changes will be shown in reverse. The box will show you your hard drive. Select the file. Then the window disappears and you appear to be back in your original file. However, if you scroll down you should begin to see red words and red lines scored

through other words. This is the redlining. Hopefully you went in the correct direction and you are seeing the latest changes in red over the original document.

3. If you realize that it is going in the "wrong" direction, i.e. it is editing out your latest changes, simply close this document WITHOUT SAVING IT. You will then be able to open the file again without redlining. Open the correct file, and select the file to compare it to as described above.

4. If you've done everything right and you are not seeing changes, it is possible your screen is not set up to show them. Try this. Under tools, select "Track Changes," then "Highlight Changes." A box will open with three boxes to choose from. Make sure the middle box is selected: "highlight changes on screen." Hit the "Okay" button, and return to your document. You should see red highlights now. If you still don't, you may accidently have selected the same two documents to compare. Close this document and repeat steps one and two again.

5. Once you have the right files being compared, and the changes are showing up on your screen, the next step is to accept or reject changes. Go back up to "Tools" in the menu bar, select "track changes" and then "accept or reject changes." A long box will appear with two boxes within it. The first is called "Changes" and it shows the name of the person who made the change, what was done and the date. The second is called "View" and there are three buttons to choose: changes with highlighting, changes without highlighting and Original. You will want to select "Changes with highlighting" On the right of the box are two "find buttons" with arrows

pointing forward and back. On the bottom are buttons to Accept, Reject, Accept All, or Reject All, Undo, and Close.

Click on the Find button with the arrow pointing forward. The first change in the document will be highlighted. Decide whether you do or don't want this change. If you want it, hit the "accept" button, and the red will disappear from the change. If you don't want it, hit the "reject" button, and the change itself will disappear. Click the find button again, and you will move to the next change. Repeat this process until you have gone through the entire document. When you are done, be sure to save the document. If you like, you can give it a new name so you know what it is.

There are times when you know you just want to accept all changes. In that case, just hit "accept all." All changes will appear in the document, without any red lines. Be sure to go back when you are complete with this document, and de-select "highlight changes on screen," or else any new work you do will appear highlighted in red.

How to quickly put all your separate chapter files into one document

When you have finished the first draft of your manuscript (chapter by chapter) you will want to put it all back together so that you can begin looking at the whole and getting the scope of it so you can look at the structural editing. Here's how to do it:

1. Open the first chapter (or the preface if that is where you are starting).

2. Go to "File" in the menu bar and select "Save As." Pick a new name for your all-in-one manuscript file—maybe "DraftwholeMS."

3. Move your cursor to the very bottom of the file. (Scroll down using the scroll bar.) Make sure to click into the very end of the file, after the last word.
4. Hit return twice.
5. Move your cursor ABOVE the last line of the file.
6. Go to "Insert" on the menu bar.
7. Select "Break" and then "Page Break." If you are in Page Layout view you will see a new page. From the Draft (or Normal) View you will see a line across the page.
8. Insert your cursor to the space BELOW the page break.
9. Type in the name or number of the next Chapter: "Chapter 2: Our Story Begins."
10. Open the second chapter.
11. Hit "Command" and "A" (Control-A for the PC) to highlight the entire text (or you can go to Edit in the Menu Bar and choose "Highlight All"
12. Hit "Command" -C (Control C for the PC) to copy all. (Or you can go to Edit in the Menu Bar and choose "Copy All." Then hit a key within the second chapter to un-highlight it (so you don't accidentally delete the entire text)
13. Move back to the first chapter. Make sure the cursor is at the bottom, below the page break.
14. Hit "Command" -V for paste. (Control V for the PC) Or you can go to Edit in the Menu Bar and choose "Paste." The entire chapter should appear.

15. Scroll down to the bottom.
16. Hit Return twice. Move the cursor ABOVE the second line. Go to Insert on the menu bar. Select "Break" and then "Page Break"
17. Move the cursor BELOW the page break.

Continue from step 9 above with each chapter until you have completed them all.

Making global changes in the manuscript

Let's say you finished your manuscript (hooray!). But you decide at the last minute to change your lead character's name from Leslie to Leah. Oh no, you think. How will I ever be able to change all those instances where I use the lead character's name? Simple. Use Find and Replace. This will work for many common changes. The one thing it won't work well for is specific grammatical changes.

Here's how to do it:

Go to "edit" in the menu bar. Select "Replace." You will see a box with two windows: Find what, and Replace with. In this case in "find" we will type "Leslie," and in "Replace" we will type "Leah." Since we are pretty sure every appearance of "Leslie" will be the lead character, we can select the "replace all" button on the bottom. This will replace every appearance of Leslie with Leah. You still may need to double-check that there aren't any Leslie's in the manuscript. You can do a search for the apostrophe, or a search for a partial on the name "Lesl" to make sure you have caught every appearance.

Miscellaneous tips for Word

- To create a new document from your keyboard:
  On the Mac
  Type "Command" N
  On the PC
  Type Control-N
- It's easier and faster to write new material in the document when it's in Draft or Normal not Page Layout view. It is especially faster to scroll through the document in Draft or Normal view. To change it, go to "View" in the menu bar and highlight Draft or Normal.
- To turn off the grammar function (so you aren't driven to distraction by Word's idea of what good writing is):

  In the menu bar choose "Word" (or in some versions "File") and then "Preferences." Pick Spelling and Grammar. If your grammar function is turned on, there will be a check mark in that box. If you click on it the checkmark will disappear. Hit enter or OK and it will apply.
- You can almost always undo the most recent thing you typed. In fact you can often continue backwards and undo in order everything you just did. Go to "Edit" in the menu bar and choose "Undo ___." It will say either "typing" or "page break" or whatever your most recent action was.

Preparing your manuscript for submission to agent

Everyone is nervous when submitting to an agent for the first time. They usually want to be assured that there is one perfect style to use, and if they use it, their manuscript will be picked up. That is not actually how it works. There are a few musts, but basically as long as you are consistent and not annoying (like choosing too many weird or hard-to-read fonts), it will be fine.

Must do:

- ✳ Print out the full manuscript
- ✳ Double space the entire manuscript
- ✳ Paginate the manuscript
- ✳ Use running heads with your name on every page
- ✳ Include your address, phone and email on the cover page
- ✳ Use the copyright symbol on the cover page:

  Title
  © by Leslie Keenan

How to print the copyright symbol:

1. Go to "Insert" in the menu bar
2. Select "Symbol"
3. Look through the chart of symbols until you see the circled c
4. Click on it, then click OK
   (You should see the circled C as above)

Note: Do not bind the manuscript. Use good paper, and use a rubber band around it. If you are mailing a large manuscript, use a manuscript box.

What typeface should you use?

Anything simple and readable. I usually use Palatino. You can also use Times, or Times New Roman.

What should your margins be set at:

Standard settings are fine—usually that's an inch top and bottom, and an inch and a quarter on the sides.

Preparing your manuscript for publication

The most important thing about preparing your manuscript for publication is that someone somewhere along the line will take your Word document and "pour" it into a design program like InDesign to lay it out in book form. Despite all the attempts Word has made to be all things, including a layout program, you really want to let the design program do the work. So you want to strip out anything fancy you may have done in the way of boxes, shading, fonts, even some headers and lists. Keep it simple. Your publisher will most likely have a protocol for you to follow, but if you keep this in mind you will have less work down the road.

Chapter 8

The Publishing Process

Explaining how book publishing works could be a book in itself—and, of course, there are many of them out there, some of which I recommend in Appendix A. In this chapter, I will give you an overview of the process and some ideas on how to decide which is the right direction to take. I have seen many changes in the publishing world and I know there are more to come. Some things, however, will always be the same.

The first important point I would like to make is this: If you are looking for outside validation that your work is good and worthwhile, you are going to be unhappy. I see many writers looking to get published by traditional publishers (read: New York publishers) as the only way they will know they are good. This is a mistake. What (New York) publishers are deciding is what they think they can sell at any particular moment in time. They may think they are deciding the value of a manuscript, but they are not. And they may also think they understand the permutations and trends of the marketplace—but my observation over the past thirty years is that they are just as likely to get it wrong as to get it right. They have certain biases—among them living in New York and thinking it is the center of the universe. I know—I lived there too. They also see a lot of manuscripts coming across their desks. What this can do is lead them to think, for instance, that there are "too many ___________________ books" out there, when in fact, the public may be clamoring for more of them. They are shocked, ten years later, when they are still selling. For instance, I once put together a book proposal about lessons I learned reading Jane Austen just around the time of the first wave of Jane Austen movies in the mid-nineties. I received many polite rejection letters claiming that the Jane Austen wave was over. Of course, this wave has continued for another fifteen years and counting, and many books about Jane Austen also succeeded. Another similar situation is publishers' attitude toward memoir. After the first wave of successful memoirs, many publishers said the trend was over and they were no longer looking for them. And yet memoirs continue to sell years later. Another mistake they often make is jumping on the bandwagon. If a book becomes a bestseller out of nowhere on a new topic, suddenly that's all they want to buy for six months—then they decide the field is crowded and don't publish anymore. This leads me to another point: You will often see articles where editors claim they are looking for this or that kind of book. Take this with a grain of salt. For the reasons just described, they could change that opinion on a dime, or be wrong.

There's one more thing to keep in mind when focusing on New York traditional publishers. Often the first reader of a manuscript—who will decide whether to pass it on to her boss—will be the lowest person on the totem pole, i.e., the assistant a year or two out of college. So the person who knows least has veto power over your manuscript.

There are many stories of truly great and/or successful writers being looked over, rejected countless times and then being successful (J.K. Rowling and the Harry Potter series, Kathryn Stockett who wrote *The Help*, William Kennedy who wrote *Ironweed*; Alex Haley, who wrote *Roots*). The best approach then is to find your validation elsewhere (hopefully inside yourself, from your supportive network of writer friends, and if you are lucky, even your family) and proceed as if this is a business—which is actually what it is. Write what you know, what you love, what your heart tells you to write. Make it the best you can (but not by being a perfectionist!). Then tell your delicate creative writer self to go mull over new ideas while your business self takes over for the next part.

The Publishing Business

When I started out in the business, there were about twenty New York publishing houses—now there are five and counting (although within each corporate structure there are many different imprints). The exciting thing is that as these publishers consolidated, smaller publishers began flourishing. Technological changes (small-run and on-demand printing presses and the Internet, for example) made it economically possible to be your own publisher as well.

Navigating this world of many options can be confusing. I will break it down for you here. The business is in flux with many changes happening quickly, so please note that for the most up-to-date information you should check my website at www.lesliekeenan.com. The rise of the kindle and other e-readers, and the success of subscription-based sites like scribd are noteable. While I will discuss them in more depth below, be aware that the most successful of these tend to be genre fiction, supported by very avid readers who review and support authors' work.

WHY FICTION IS DIFFERENT

Fiction is basically sold by word of mouth. Someone reads the book and recommends it to someone else. It requires time and commitment.

People are reluctant to commit without a payoff, so they look to a) their favorite authors; b) books recommended by their favorite authors; c) books recommended by friends; d) books recommended by reviewers they like; or e) and f) books recommended by bookstore owners or librarians. Traditional publishing is well-suited to reaching this market. The editor who acquires a fiction title is usually known to book sellers. A sales rep trusts the editor and believes it's good, hand sells it to the bookstore, and the bookstore hand sells it to a customer. Or, a reviewer at *Kirkus Review* or *Publisher's Weekly* likes the books from Knopf or Algonquin and reads those before others received and gives a starred review. The reviewer for the *New York Times* sees that, reads it too, and gives it a rave. The bookstores read it, rave, and sell it to you. It is difficult for small or self-publishers to break in, and it can take awhile to develop credibility. Nonfiction is much different. You can understand it by its title, or by flipping through it in a bookstore. It doesn't require as big a commitment.

If you are writing nonfiction, all options are open to you. Read through this chapter and begin thinking about your own abilities and interests, and take the quiz below to decide if you are a good candidate for self-publishing. Mainstream fiction (see box) has to be published in more traditional means

– major houses, some smaller presses and university presses. (And if you are writing a memoir, it will actually be sold more like fiction than nonfiction, so you should follow the protocol for fiction.) You should begin with Traditional Publishing for Fiction, below. Unless you are an excellent candidate for self-publishing (see the Self-Publishing Questionnaire below to determine this), I recommend you use the approach that I took as an agent. Start at the top and work your way down. The "top" meant publishers who paid the most and responded the quickest—the top six publishers. This was the "A" list. The "B" list consisted of publishers who might not respond as quickly, and the "C" list included publishers who might not even give an advance, but would commit to keep the book in print. If you are not able to find someone interested in publishing your work, then you can look at the self-publishing options.

Traditional Publishing for Nonfiction

First, you need an agent. Even many of the smaller publishers who used to review unsolicited manuscripts now require an agent. By doing this, the publishers are letting the agents be the ones to review all the manuscripts and do the pre-screening for them. Agents are willing to do it to find the gold hidden in a stack of unknowns. Remember, agents' fortunes are tied to the authors fortunes (they receive a commission based on advance and sales of the books of the authors they represent).

If you are writing non-fiction, the good news is that your book doesn't have to be finished in order to get an agent, a publisher, and perhaps even an advance. You can write a book proposal first. A book proposal is really a mini-business plan for your book.

How to Write a Book Proposal

I am about to tell you everything you need to know about writing a book proposal. There are also entire books (many of them) describing this process as well. Some are recommended in Appendix A. I will give you this caution: Many authors are trying to find the *magic formula* that will get their book acquired by an agent, editor, or publisher. The truth is, though, there is no magic formula for a book proposal. It doesn't have to be a particular format, font, size. It has to be consistent in format, it has to be clear, and it has to cover certain ground. Beyond that, it is an individual matter. I once saw a proposal that broke every rule in the book, yet it was compelling and told the story of the book, and how it would be promoted, extremely well. It received a six-figure advance.

A standard book proposal should have these sections:

The Overview

A two-to-three page description of the book idea, written to the editor, explaining why this is the best idea ever, and showing the market. Its purpose is to get the editor excited and eager to know more.

About the Author

From one or two paragraphs up to a page of description of who you are: your credentials and a little of your story (i.e., why you are writing the book).

Market

One or two pages that clearly and specifically delineate who you think the market for the book is. People often think broader is better (larger audience=more sales). The reverse is true. A targeted, narrow audience is much easier to find and sell to. Use facts, statistics, and numbers where you have them to be clear on who the market is. By "market" I mean the audience who will want this book. This is the left-brained section of the proposal. The more specific and realistic you are, the better. For instance, when writing the book proposal for my sister's book, we determined the audience was parents of kids with allergies. We had a statistic that a certain percentage of children have allergies. We looked up the census data to see how many children there were who were under 18 at the last census, and used the actual number of thousands of children who had allergies.

Like Books

A subset of the marketing section. This is a bibliographical listing of similar titles that, in one or two sentences, explains the book and its difference from your proposed book. Any sales figures you have should be included. In writing this section, you need to balance between wanting to show that there is a market for your subject (many books on the topic, and they all sell), and wanting to show that yours is the only one out there (there aren't too many books out there yet). You want the perfect balance between too many and none.

Finding real sales figures can be a problem. Sometimes you can find the figures for how many books are in print on the back of the paperback version of a book. You can also cite bestseller lists if there are any. Sometimes you can find references to actual sales numbers in a "round-up" edition of Publisher's Weekly that reviews the previous year's sales (this issue comes out in January or February of the following year). Libraries almost always carry back issues of Publisher's Weekly.

Publicity

This section should be included if you plan to do your own marketing of yourself and your project. It should contain a detailed description of your marketing plan - how much money you will spend, the cities you will go to and/or the level of your current activity (workshops and speaking engagements, Internet presence, etc.) - and how you will increase it when the book is published. Any previous publicity on you or your idea should also be included.

Annotated Table of Contents

This is a list of each chapter you plan to write and a paragraph or two describing the planned contents of each. (You can write up to a page on each chapter if it's necessary, but no more.) Focus on giving the editor a clear sense of the material. Be specific, and don't fudge. You especially want to leave them with the feeling that there's a lot of solid material in your work. An editor reads the sample chapter to determine the quality of your writing, but looks here to see what it is you are actually saying.

Sample Chapter

One complete chapter of the book must be included. It should be the most dramatic or important chapter of the book. Often it is the first chapter, but not always. If the book is very long, or there are many different things to be covered, it can be helpful to include two chapters that convey the breadth of the material.

That's it! That's all you need to have. Of course, it sounds simple and I promise you it will be much harder to write than the book itself. Practice the same techniques I gave you earlier in the book for writing your manuscript. Also, give yourself permission to write a lot out, then go back and cut it to the appropriate length.

How to Create Your "Pitch"

If you work on your "pitch" around the same time you write the proposal, you will have a leg up with each. Sometimes you will get clear on what your pitch is through writing out the overview of your proposal. What you want to be able to do is say in one sentence what your book is in a way that people will immediately understand—and hopefully be excited by. What do I mean?

Let's look at some examples. In *The New York Times* the description of the Harry Potter series goes like this: A wizard hones his conjuring skills in the service of fighting evil.

A much more exciting description can be found on the web: A boy wizard begins training and must battle for his life with the Dark Lord who murdered his parents.

Notice that while the first version is factual, the second version pulls us in more because we see what is at stake—it's personal.

You want to convey something of the book in a way that makes sense to people. Often that will mean comparing it to another book or movie people know well.

A movie pitch that worked went like this: *Jaws* in space. The movie was Alien.

Here is Moby Dick in one sentence: "An obsessed sea captain hunts the white whale who has taken his leg, to the disaster of all aboard the ship."

There's a humorous version of it: Everyone dies except fish and Ish.

Here are a few alternates for *Gone With the Wind* that I wrote to show how you can switch the focus if you like:

A vivacious Southern Belle is forced to do whatever it takes to survive the Civil War and its aftermath, inadvertently throwing away the only man who is a match for her in the process.

Set in the collapse of the Old South, a Southern Belle does whatever it takes to survive, all the while her stubborn devotion to the wrong man ruins her chances for happiness with the right man.

You can focus on the setting, the history, the struggle to survive, or the romance of the story.

I first developed my ability to sum up a book in one line when I was an editorial assistant at *Book-of-the-Month Club* and one of my jobs was typing the notes for the editorial meeting—which consisted of lists of books and one-line descriptions. When you have about a half hour (and are using an IBM Selectric III typewriter—not a computer!), you learn to think quickly and get to the point.

The simplest way to approach it is to start writing. Write as if you are talking and write a page or two. Print them out. Read it over and circle any lines or phrases you think are interesting. Type those in a new page. Rework it. Treat it like a puzzle and just move phrases around, changing up the order in ways you wouldn't normally think of. Try to get the essence of the book down to a paragraph and then shorten that. It is also *really* helpful to ask people what they think. It goes without saying that these should be nice, helpful, supportive people you trust (see the list on how to select a good and appropriate reader in Chapter 5: Editing Your First Draft).

One of my favorites is a quick line I developed for a client: Bridget Jones at an ashram. It tells you exactly what it is.

A lot of self-help books use their pitch as their title: *How to Win Friends and Influence People* is a classic example. A more recent one is *The Life-Changing Magic of Tidying Up*. It tells what it is in an unexpected way ("magic," "tidying," and "life-changing" are not typically used for organizing books. Here the word organizing doesn't come until the subtitle—

The Japanese Art of Decluttering and Organizing.).

Once your book proposal is done, it's time to find an agent. Contrary to what you might think, agents are always on the look-out for the next great book. Most people in publishing are in it for love, and are really wanting to fall in love with a new project. What they don't like is having their time wasted by people who are unprofessional, annoying, or haven't done their homework.

How to Make Yourself Irresistible to An Agent

1. Have a great idea.

Every agent looks for the next great idea. While there is increasing emphasis on the market portion of this equation, (see #5), a good idea still sells.

2. Be passionate about it.

It is true that authors sell books. Authors are always the spokespeople for their product–'the book'–and the degree of their passion determines the level of sales.

3. Have a complete proposal and at least one complete chapter for the agent to consider.

Another phrase for this is do your homework. It's not enough just to have thought of the idea; words need to be on paper, and in a clear, concise, easy-to-read format.

4. Understand the agent's needs and time constraints.

While agents are always looking for good authors and good projects to sell, there are many time constraints. Looking for and developing new projects and supporting the author is only part of an agent's job. At least 50% of their time is focused on discerning the needs of the editors they sell to. Additionally, every agent and editor in publishing is continually inundated with manuscripts from unpublished authors. Don't become another drain on their precious time.

5. Have a clear, developed market, and be reaching it consistently already.

If you've done this part correctly, the agent will be calling you. An article about you in the *New York Times* always sparks interest. Barring that, local media interest, consistent workshops or classes, a definite internet following and signs that you can increase your market to a national level is what agents look for. I will be developing this further below.

One day I was settling down to read a *New York Times* article I saw was the most emailed on the website several days in a row. It was long. I got to the end of the first page and thought, this is a marvelous piece. So heartfelt, yet factual, combining personal story and national trends. Who wrote it? I looked back up to the top of the page and saw it was a friend of mine! I emailed my congratulations and she emailed back that she was overwhelmed with a deadline for a book proposal. Hmm. Had it anything to do with the article, I wanted to know. Yes, an agent became interested after the article came out and she was finishing the book proposal for her. She went on to get a hefty advance.

Where to Start to Look for An Agent

The first place you must turn to for an agent is the place writers hate to go. You must ask your friends and family if they know anyone who has an agent. You probably already know someone who does. Then you have to ask them if they can tell you who it is. Yes, this is the time to call in favors. The most ideal recommendation an agent can receive is for one of their published authors to tell them, "I have a friend who is great and you must look at her proposal." This is even more highly valued than if another person in publishing recommends someone (since the friend has nothing at all to gain from referring you). If you are not quite that close to the person you or someone you know knows, just the name and phone or email is a good start.

The second best way to get an agent is to meet one at a writers' conference. This is in fact the main reason to go to a writers' conference. Agents who attend these conferences are actively looking for new clients. That is why *they* go. And often they will read a few pages of writers' work as part of the conference (sometimes for an extra fee). So how do you decide if it's worth the money to go to a particular conference? First and foremost, are you ready? Do you have your pitch? Have you written your proposal? Do you feel confident enough in yourself? It's okay if you aren't ready yet. Just keep working on the book and invest the money later when you are ready. But, let's say you think you are ready. Look up the various writers' conferences. Look to see what agents (and possibly editors) will be there. Do they acquire books like yours? Will you be able to meet them at this conference? If so, then yes, go. And make sure not to hold back. You must introduce yourself and your work. I know this is something all writers (or I should say most) hate to do. But remember, this is the reason the agent is there too. If you follow the guidelines I laid out above, the agent should be happy to talk to you.

Other Places to Look for An Agent

Let's say you don't know anyone who has an agent, and a writers' conference is out of your reach for now. What do you do? Don't worry, there are lots of ways to find the right agent. First, start noticing your favorite books and begin making a habit of turning to the acknowledgments page and see if the author thanks their agent by name (most do). Sometimes you won't know which is the agent, but often they are acknowledged that way. Begin compiling a list. You will tend to like books that relate in some way to the one you are writing, and the agent who represents these kinds of books is more likely to appreciate yours. You can add to that list when you read about a particular agent online or in newspapers or magazines. You can also pay attention to the trade publications. The traditional one is *Publishers Weekly*, which is no longer as current as a website called Publishers Marketplace (which has a free daily email called Publishers Lunch). A word of caution: I don't actually recommend you subscribe to either of these because it is easy to become overwhelmed and to feel, as writers tend to do, that there are so many books already out there, no one will want mine. So my caution is only go to these sites when you are ready, and do research. If you want to subscribe, Publishers Marketplace allows you to actually search recent deals by subject and by agent so you can see the kinds of books agents represent and the number of deals they do. (But another word of caution, some of the top name agents don't bother reporting their deal information because they have no need to.) They also compile a yearly book that contains all these lists, which may be more economical although it goes out of date fairly quickly. Additionally, there are many books out there that attempt to fill this need of matching writers and agents. The biggest problem is that they too go out of date quickly. Some, however, can be helpful and useful. See Appendix A.

How to Submit Your Manuscript to Agents

Once you have a list of five to ten names of possible agents, do your homework again. Most agents today have websites that include submission guidelines. If not, go to your local library's reference section and ask for the *Literary Marketplace* (LMP), which has a complete list of agents and instructions on how to submit. Follow them carefully. This is your first test. Can you pay attention and do as asked? Some will want a query first (meaning a letter only), some will want a query and proposal, some will want a query and the first fifty pages. Make sure to provide what the agent wants. Some will only want email, some will only want mail. Prepare this as required, and submit up to ten at a time. This is standard in the industry, as long as you let each agent know "this is a multiple submission." The only exception to this rule is children's books. In that end of the business most agents request single submission. That is, you send to each agent one at a time and wait for a response before submitting to the next.

How to Evaluate Whether This Agent Is Right for You

What? I don't just eagerly accept any agent who wants me? No, you interview them too. A bad agent can actually make things worse.

How to recognize sharks:

* They ask for a fee to read your work (more than just paying copying and postage during the submission process, which is standard but shouldn't be paid until the proposal is actually being submitted to editors).
* They say they want to represent you but want you to work with an editor that they recommend first. (Some legitimate agents do this too, but it can be a kickback scheme.)
* They aren't a member of the Association of Authors' Representatives (AAR) or listed in the LMP.

- They place internet ads. (Most legitimate agents have no need to advertise for authors.)

Questions to ask:

- What are some recent deals you have done?
- What plans do you have for submitting my book?
- When do you plan on sending it out?
- How available will you be for me during this process?

A good agent has already thought of what to do while reading your proposal, and is also willing to be upfront about it. It's also a very good idea to get clear at the outset how often you will be able to talk with your agent. The top agents will often assign someone else in the office to be your point person, while they spend their time selling your book to editors. Make sure you will be comfortable with that. There are other agents who are more hands-on and want to work with you on the proposal and even other ideas. Get clear yourself about what style you want, and be direct about it.

I once had a client who had two agents interested in her. One was among the top agents in the country; another was a young up-and-comer. My client decided she wanted the more intimate relationship offered by the younger agent than the prestige of the top agent (whom she would not get to speak with regularly).

The Contract

Once you have found the right agent, you will want a contract. In the publishing business there are some agents who are a little loose about this, and out of enthusiasm might start selling your project before the agreement is signed. Your ideal is to have a contract for this title only, and that the rights revert to you in six months or a year, if the agent hasn't sold it. A student once told me of her father-in-law, who had an agent who was not doing a thing for a year. The father-in-law went directly to a publisher and got a deal but was sued and lost the case because there was no deadline in the contract.

Some agents only want to work with you if they get to do all your projects. That's okay too as long as you are both clear. It is totally okay and very common for the agent to charge you for the costs of copying, mailing and telephone. Make sure there's a limit specified in the contract, usually about $200 without approval.

Then the decision about which publishers to submit to is a discussion you have with your agent. And since you have picked a good agent whom you trust, you leave most of the decision-making to her!

How to Have a Happy Relationship with Your Editor/ Publisher/In-house Publicist

You may have thought at the beginning of this process that the end goal was getting the publisher. Ask most published authors and they will tell you, no, that's just the beginning. Ideally, you want a publisher who is working with you to promote your book, and an editor who answers your calls and is eager to sign up your next book. I hope that is what happens, but I have heard a few horror stories too. Here's what you can do to get the best possible outcome:

First, as with the agent, understand the time constraints of everyone in publishing. They are juggling lots of books and authors, and you can help them by being courteous and helpful and responsive (but not a doormat either). If you have been doing all the homework I suggest here, you already have a "platform" you are reaching, and you and the publisher work together to get the word out when the book is released.

BASED ON $20 6X9 PB BOOK OF 250 PP			
	Traditional Publisher	**Small Publisher**	**Self-Publisher**
Royalty	15% or $3 per book (hardcover); 7.5% or $1.50 per book (paperback)	15% of net or $1.50 per book (assumes average 50% discount to stores)	Profit after expenses—Assume $10,000 in pre-press costs and $3.85 mfg. in on-demand
Wholesale royalty	7.5% of $10 or $.75 if hardcover; 3.75% of $10 or $.38 if paperback	Same	Amazon discount of 40% or $8.15 per book with all costs deducted
Volume sales	Varies	Same	Same
If you sell 10,000 you earn:	$15,000 at top royalty; $3800 at low	$15,000	All through Amazon: $71,500

Beyond the Top New York Publishers

B-list publishers pay less up front than traditional publishers, and also respond more slowly to queries. Some require agents, some don't. They also may pay you royalties differently. C-list publishers may not pay an advance at all, and yet they may still be the best option for you, because they look on you as a partner, and may work harder and keep your book in print longer . There are also co-publishers, and self-publishing. In order to make the best decision about which kind of publisher to go with, it will help to review the overall economics of publishing.

The Economics of Publishing

The reality of publishing is that it is a complex business with narrow margins, and it's not a place you usually find easy money. That is, if your goal is to make a million dollars, this may not be where you want to start.

I have created a chart which is very rough using some basic assumptions to give you a framework for understanding the different choices, assuming a $20 6 x 9 trade paperback book of 250 pages. (Note I'm not looking at ebooks here.)

When you look at it this way, you may say, "Well, clearly self-publishing is the way to go!" I wanted to show the dramatic difference in receiving a share of the profit versus a royalty; however, the caveat here is that I am assuming you can sell 10,000 copies on your own as well as through a publisher. That is a big if. But if you have to do all the marketing yourself anyway, and you are a self-starter who is good at it and knows your audience and can reach them, you may want to pick this route. (You can refer to the marketing section below for a starting point on how to market your book.)

SELF-PUBLISHING QUESTIONAIRE

I am a self-starter

❏ yes ❏ no

I have strong opinions about the cover and interior design

❏ yes ❏ no

I have a clear defined audience

❏ yes ❏ no

I know where to find them

❏ yes ❏ no

There's a compelling reason the book needs to come out quickly

❏ yes ❏ no

I have devised a questionnaire to see if you are a good candidate for self-publishing.

If you say yes to three of these, you may want to consider self-publishing seriously. If you do, remember that having a finished book is one thing, getting it sold is another. There are on-demand publishers who have tried to be one-stop-shopping for authors, providing editorial assistance and design; they don't, however, provide real distribution. I also don't think many of them leave you with a high enough percentage to make a profit (I am thinking specifically of Lulu.com and iuniverse). Also keep in mind that many independent bookstores refuse to carry those books. (If you know your audience, you may be able to bypass bookstores entirely, so this may not be an issue. However, do look the numbers over carefully before committing.)

Some people have self-published their book with an eye to having a traditional publisher take it over once they have proven that there is an audience. (It's easier to do this if you focus on a narrower geographical area, because fewer sales are required.) *Rich Dad, Poor Dad* by Robert Kiyosaki is an example of this. The author (a marketer who was already teaching seminars on the subject) self-published, and after sales reached a certain level, Warner Books swooped in and acquired the rights and made it a national bestseller.

There is another option in between smaller presses and self-publishing. That is co-publishing. Co-publishers *are* publishers, and their logo appears on the spine, but you share in the proceeds. Co-publishers provide the expertise, and often ask the author to provide the upfront money for publication, and then the profit is split usually 50/50. This can work if you don't want to have to become a publisher, but you have answered yes to at least three of the questions in the questionnaire above.

On the next page is another chart that lays out the reasons to choose different kinds of publishing:

E-books

Advances in technology have also created a real market for ebooks—books that can be read electronically by an ereader—like Amazon's Kindle, Barnes & Noble's Nook, the Apple iPad, or the Kobo, among others. They can also usually be read by any computer with the right software. (I am not referring here to the downloadable PDF's that are also often called ebooks, but are meant to be printed out to be read, or read on a computer.) While traditional publishers have been converting their titles to this format, many writers who were not having success getting their titles published have gone directly to ebooks on their own, thus keeping the profit for themselves.

PUBLISHING CHOICE PROS & CONS

Traditional Publisher	Small Publisher	Self-Publishing	Co-Publishing
		Reasons to Choose	
Up front advance, wide distribution	You don't have to pay upfront Prestige distribution	Total control Learning curve is steep Much higher profit margins	Expertise Want to self-publish but don't want to be the publisher
		Reasons Not to Choose	
Lowest amount earned per book	Lower profit	You have to do all the work yourself and also put up all the money. Learning curve is steep.	You have to do some of the work and advance some/all of the money

As ereaders have grown in popularity, the sales of ebooks have risen, and many stories have appeared in the mainstream media about their success. The most well-known of these is the story of Amanda Hocking, who wrote a young adult vampire romance called *My Blood Approves*. She got rejections from New York publishers. So in April 2010 she uploaded it to the Amazon Kindle and then with Smashwords, which uploaded it to Nook, Kobo, and others. The book started selling so she wrote more books. By June of that year she sold 6,000 books in one day. Her sales kept increasing until she sold over 100,000 books in one day in January 2011. Two months later she received a $2 million advance from St. Martin's Press for four new titles, and they also reissued the ebooks in paperback.

Another well-known story is of Hugh Howey, who wrote a science fiction series. He did not try any New York publishers, instead choosing the self-publishing route, focusing on ebooks, and priced them very low (99 cents). At one point he was generating $30,000 to $40,000 a month in sales. He turned down many seven figure offers from publishers, until finally accepting a mid-six figure deal with Simon & Schuster—for just the print rights to his books.

It seems to be true (and both these examples demonstrate) that the ebooks that sell best are the kind of books that were formerly sold as mass market paperbacks—romance novels, science fiction, and fantasy, particularly those geared to younger readers. (It makes sense if you think about it as an impulse buy.) And even the most successful of these have chosen to go with a traditional publisher after they have success—since it still makes sense to cover *all* markets.

It would seem to me then, that the best strategy is to consider ebooks alongside traditional, small, and self- or co-publishing. There are lower overhead costs since an e-file requires no production costs, but there are still pre-press costs like editing, type design (not essential but helpful), cover design and file conversion.

The economics of ebooks change rapidly. Amazon will give a higher percentage of the sale price to the author if the title is exclusive with them, and has the price point they set (very low). The main point is that while the cost is lower, if you do it yourself there is no one else to share it with, so the author could end up making more than in the traditional publishing world.

Traditional Publishing for Fiction

The strategy for getting fiction published is different. As I said earlier, fiction requires a larger commitment, and so most people want some assurance before they begin that they will like the book. Usually that is a recommendation from a trusted source—typically a friend, a favorite author, or someone whose opinion they know and trust. The first step, then, to being recommended (whether to an agent, an editor, or your ultimate reader) is to be chosen by a known quantity. If you are writing literary fiction, literary magazines are the answer. Submitting smaller pieces of your writing (and creating new writing just for this purpose) is a way to get your name out. Another way is to go to the right writing workshops (read the material about the workshop and who is leading classes there—look for people who have worked on books you like and respect) and get read by people in the field. Actually getting an MFA is another route, although the most expensive. Whatever method you choose, befriend other writers, and network. The way literary fiction is sold is basically by one person reading it and recommending it to another. You can't judge without reading. It's a very personal, intimate process. Submit your work to contests and for literary prizes . You could consider using Writers' Relief or another author's submission service to assist you in this process. (They need to accept you, and they charge you a fee to recommend places for you to submit; they send you the addresses and you do the mailing.)

Fiction is also different because you must complete your manuscript before an agent or an editor will consider you. This is because first, the agent or editor needs to know that you can finish a manuscript, and second, they need to know that they like the plot and the way it ends. Usually an agent will ask for a synopsis and the first 50 pages of the manuscript. This allows them to evaluate two things: the plot or storyline, and the quality of your writing. And, it allows them to do so without sitting down to read all 500 pages of your precious manuscript. (Think about how much time it would take if an agent did that with every manuscript submitted!)

Commercial fiction is easier to break into than literary fiction. The primary purpose of commercial fiction is to entertain. Literary fiction challenges and demands a deeper level of attention. Great authors did both: Shakespeare, Dickens, Tolstoy. Others were once defined one way (Jane Austen was considered commercial) and became identified as another (now her books are acknowledged as literature). Commercial fiction is a bit less subjective than literary fiction. It tells a good story. If it falls inside a genre (like mystery, romance, science fiction, or fantasy), it's even easier to break into. Genre follows a defined formula and doesn't deviate from it. Even these can rise to literature (Raymond Chandler, Ray Bradbury, Philip K. Dick, Elizabeth Peters). For some reason, mystery writers and romance writers are much more supportive of each other than literary authors are. There are great conferences to attend and agents are out there searching for you more actively. If this is you, I recommend you pick a good conference and go; make connections and stay connected. Work on your pitch. (See How to Create Your "Pitch," above.)

How to Create A Marketing Platform

Whatever level of publishing you have decided to pursue, and whether you are writing fiction or nonfiction, you want the readers who are looking for your book to be able to find you and your book. The Internet has changed everything in terms of how authors and readers can connect. Whereas in the past you had to go through a long chain of people to get to the bookstore, where your reader would have to walk in and go to the shelf to find your book, today you can talk directly to your reader on the Internet. (This is true whether you are publishing traditionally, self-publishing or doing an e-book.) So how do you do that? The first thing you want to do is think about who your reader is. Hopefully you already have a sense of this because it has informed everything about the writing of the book. You want to get more specific, not more general. While everyone in the country (or the world) may be a potential audience for your book, it's actually more helpful to think that new college graduates are who you want to focus on, or first-time parents, or teen readers of fantasy novels. Then you can think about where these readers may already be hanging out online, and begin interacting with them there. Below are some suggestions for ways and places to do that. The Internet changes quickly so this list is necessarily incomplete.

Blogging

I start with blogging since to my mind it's the most natural and compelling for a writer. After all, it is writing, and you can stay safely in your own house and not even have to get out of your pj's! There are many sites today (such as WordPress) that make it easy for you to create your own blog and begin writing. What is harder is thinking about what to write, how often, and when. I find it's much easier to limit yourself to a topic and a time frame, at least in the beginning. One of my students decided to write about her daughter in high school. The famous blog that became the book and movie *Julie and Julia* had a hook that made people want to follow it—the author was writing about cooking every recipe from Julia Child's *The Art of French Cooking* over the course of one year.

Another issue is what kind of writing you are doing. Since writing is your profession and not just a hobby, I recommend writing about your writing, or exploring ideas within the blog, but saving polished, finished pieces for publication elsewhere. (Note that many magazines will not accept work that has already been made available online.) Blogging is really more like a public diary and can be more immediate and spontaneous than finished writing.

Finally, once you commit to blogging, you also need to commit to doing it regularly. Once a week is fine, even twice a month is fine, but be consistent so your followers will know what to expect. And don't forget to respond to comments you receive! Your responsiveness is what will eventually lead to the "marketing platform."

Tumblr (and probably some other sites) actually falls under blogging for our purposes. Tumblr just makes it very easy for novices to combine images and video right into the blog. You can check out the site and see if it appeals to you. One word of caution: It's actually best to keep a home blogging site in addition to using one of these others because they are proprietary and if they shut down, you lose everything you put up on that site.

Facebook

You may already be on Facebook. In addition to your personal Facebook account, you can create Pages on Facebook that are intended for businesses. The most common way that authors use Pages is to create a Page for themselves as "author," and/or a Page for the book. There are two differences between your personal Facebook profile and the Page. Anyone can see and follow your Page, but must be invited to see your personal profile. And anyone can post to your Page.

If you are just starting to write, you can still have an author

Page on Facebook. You can share about your adventures in writing. One former student of mine shares photos of locations she is writing about in her historical novel. She has also shared interesting articles about the time period she writes about.

Twitter

Twitter lets you write short messages in 140 characters. It is a form of broadcasting; that is, the conversation only goes one way. You send out the message, and your followers can read it. They may want to respond to your tweet, or they may choose to "retweet" your tweet to all their followers. What's cool about Twitter is that anyone can follow you, and you can follow anyone. Famous people have thousands of followers. But smaller numbers of dedicated followers can be a firm foundation for a marketing platform.

Twitter can also be a good form for writers. It's a bit like haiku. Can you say something interesting, creative or funny in that small space? If you can consistently do that, or interestingly "curate" good information (that means sharing interesting articles from all over the Internet, or sharing powerful quotes), you can develop a following. This may be easier than you think. It simply means to link to articles on your topic, whatever it is. On my Twitter feed, I "retweet" articles related to writing or publishing. But I only retweet ones I have read and like. People will begin to see that you are worth following, and follow you and/or retweet your retweets.

If you have a good sense of humor (Beware: It has to be really good and it's easy to offend.), you can see if you can write a good joke on a hot topic. Many comedians have done this to great success. For instance, after word spread that Kim Kardashian and Kanye West named their baby "North West," Mo Rocca had a very clever tweet:

"And that's pretty much all the guidance she can expect."

The deeper point here is that writing, observation, and storytelling are what works on Twitter as well as the other platforms, and these are skills you already have.

The other powerful thing about Twitter is that you can develop relationships easily with people you don't know. So, let's say you are a writer of mysteries and your favorite author is on Twitter. You can begin by following her, and then occasionally responding to something she writes. She may be intrigued enough to follow you, and a few years down the road may be happy to read your manuscript.

Linked In

Linked In started out as a website for job seekers to post resumes. Gradually it has become more like Facebook, where people can network and share ideas, but it still has more of a business caste to it. It can be useful for writers, especially writers of non-fiction. If you are already on Linked In for business, you can add writer to your list of skills. The main feature of Linked In is that you can find and be introduced to people you have been looking to connect with. Once you have connected with your network, Linked In shows you how many "links" connect you to the person you want to reach. So it may be that you are one link away (a friend is a friend of that person). This can come in handy if you want to ask someone for an endorsement, or if you want to interview someone for research.

Another possible use of Linked In is in its Groups feature. You can join a group that relates to your field, and then be helpful within that group. Let's say you have a technique that helps self-employed people be more productive. You find a group for self-employed people (maybe a user group for specific industries) and you help them for free; they learn about you and your book and spread the word.

Pinterest

Pinterest has become increasingly popular, particularly with women. It is a site that makes "pinning" photos from anywhere around the web simple. You create your own "boards" and then pin pictures to them, a little like making a collage. It's great of course for fashion and food, and also for ideas for kids' projects. If your book has any visuals, this could be a great place to expose them. Another obvious idea for writers is quotes. There's a very easy way to turn your quotes (your own from your book, or others' that are included in your book) into visual posters that are easy to share. The cool thing about Pinterest is that anyone can easily find the originator of posts no matter how many times it's shared. So they can quickly get linked back to you, and then to your website.

You Tube

OK, you may think the idea of having a You Tube channel is over the top, but bear with me. Video is becoming more and more popular on the web. And since you are a writer and therefore have "content" (what writers prefer to call stories and ideas to share), you now have another form in which to share and reach an audience. There are a few ways to approach this. One is to hire a professional to interview you about your book, and then post it on You Tube and imbed the link on your website as another way for potential readers to get to know you. Another is to do the homespun method of creating your own video using simple technology on your computer.

You can treat the video like a blog, and keep doing more of them over a period of time, in sequence. This can work well if you are writing a nonfiction book about a topic that is informational. The main thing to focus on is the content–what it is you have to say. Then figure out the best way to say that visually in three minutes or less.

Many authors feel intimidated or overwhelmed by the prospect of doing all this work. My suggestion is to break it down into small, manageable pieces that seem fun to you. Take it slow, and do it at a time other than your scheduled writing time. Remember that the point of this is to find out where your potential readers are on the web, and begin connecting with them. The Internet is just a new place to be doing the same things authors have been doing for hundreds of years.

Here are two examples of writers who began with blogs and ended up with traditional publishers.

Alan Sepinwall, who is a television critic, and one of my favorite bloggers, self-published a book (*The Revolution Was Televised)* in the fall of 2012. I emailed him to ask why he had decided to go this route and not the traditional one. I assumed someone with his high profile (he has a large and developed online following after 15 years of blogging) would not have trouble finding a publisher. He directed me to an interview he did online with Indie Reader (http://indiereader.com/2012/12/5-questions-for-the-2nd-indie-author-to-break-the-sound-barrier/) wherein he explained that while he had initially attempted to go through traditional means, and had received a small offer, he decided he'd do better on his own. And then, apparently to his surprise as well as everyone else's, Michiko Kakutani, the feared *New York Times* book reviewer, gave him a rave review (Dec. 6, 2012). (http://www.nytimes.com/2012/12/04/books/the-revolution-was-televised-by-alan-sepinwall.html?pagewanted=all&_r=0)

Most of the time, even books from major publishers can't get attention from her, so for her to review a self-published book was big news. And his comment in the Indie Reader interview was telling:

"There are tools for self-publishing — in terms of production, distribution and promotion — that didn't used to exist. (One of the most frequent comments I got from people right after the paperback came out was, 'It looks like a real book' — by which they meant, it looked exactly like a book they would find on the shelf at Barnes & Noble.) And I suppose in that way, the rise of the cable networks — who, by the late '90s, were able to make shows that looked like 'real' TV shows — parallels what's happening here."

The story could end there, with a happy self-published author. But then, the first week of January 2013, I noticed something on the Publishers Marketplace website—the record of a deal between Sepinwall and Touchstone Publishing. He sold the rights to his book (through an agency by the way) to a mainstream publisher!

Another writer, who was not a journalist first, started a blog called Honest Toddler. She developed a following among parents who shared the screamingly funny posts. She used Facebook and Twitter to support the posts and build her following. She was picked up by Huffington Post, and mentioned in a few mainstream publications. And next thing you know, she had a book deal with a mainstream publisher.

Major publishers want you to already have a base audience; the book is an afterthought, another product to sell to people who already know you. For some people—who speak to large audiences as part of their job—this is possible. For example, motivational speakers. New age networks can work like this too. Carolyn Myss is one example.

For you at this stage, the book is the point, and you want to build the audience through and with it. Don't despair. This is possible. You can start where you are and build from there.

The moral? There's no one way. Every situation is unique and you must consider all the variables. In Sepinwall's case, he had a strong following, and lots of connections in the blogosphere to build interest in the beginning, and then he decided to capitalize on the publicity and get out of the self-publishing business all at once. Honest Toddler was probably always more interested in a mainstream publisher (she, after all, was busy with a toddler).

The Real World

While the ability to connect on the internet is a powerful tool, sometimes nothing replaces the old-fashioned, in-person connection. It turns out there are several things in the real, non-internet world you can be doing to support your book (whether it is complete or not). These are more readily applicable to non-fiction, but they can apply to fiction as well. First, think of joining organizations that relate to your field. But don't just join, attend meetings, meet people, and talk about your common interest (which should relate to your book). For fiction writers, organizations that focus on your niche are a great place to start (like Sisters in Crime if you are a female mystery writer). These real connections will help you in the future. Then, think about any topic you can give talks on that would be appropriate for local groups. Many groups actually need and want speakers for their meetings, and getting started this way is easier than national groups, and can help you learn what people respond to.

If speaking doesn't come naturally to you, think about joining Toastmasters, which has branches across the country and is a very supportive environment to begin to practice. And don't forget that the real connections you make here can also help you down the line. Finally, don't forget two places where you might already spend a good deal of time: your local library and bookstore. Befriend the librarian and someone at the bookstore, mention what you are writing about, and lay the groundwork for when you may want to give a talk when your book is out. Keep in mind that libraries often like to have speakers on relevant topics, so they might have you before your book is done.

Whatever your particular path to connecting with your readers, you will need to balance the business of publishing with your creative writing time. It may work best at this stage to commit a certain amount of time each week to the business end, and a certain amount for writing. See the next chapter for where the writing journey goes next.

Meanwhile, can you commit to doing the business of writing this week? Can you commit to creative writing time this week?

Chapter 9 

What's Next?

Congratulations! You finished your manuscript (or at least you are willing to believe it's possible, which is why you have turned to this chapter). After the initial thrill and relief, you might be wondering, what now?

You might already have a long list of tasks to be involved with. You might be one of the people who had a second book tucked into the first that you know you want to be working on now. Or, you are planning a sequel to this one. Or, you may be afraid you only had one book in you and you don't want to confirm that.

Whatever category you fall into right now, I want you to appreciate that the space you are in now is the most important in the creative process—and the most misunderstood and unacknowledged. It is the fallow period, the time between. Many people think of creativity as that white heat when ideas are coming to you, or the ease of flow when the writing comes pouring out. But actually, this fallow place is the most powerful. The unknown, the void, is where new ideas come from. But you have to trust the uncertainty, and "hold the space" for it to come in.

Our culture is so biased against this that some people would accuse you of wasting time or daydreaming or loafing. You may be denounced as a bum. From the outside, it can look like nothing is happening, and that's scary. The temptation is great to fill the void with a lot of activity that is really just busy work.

Here's what I'd like to suggest you do instead, especially if you think you only have one book in you (but also give it a try even if you think you *do* know what's next). Keep the writing schedule you were working with. Go to the same place you were going (your office, a café, the corner spot in your living room). Show up. And then sit. Sit and stare into space. Or let yourself read something you have wanted to read. Look over ideas you may already have. Just be there. If it's really uncomfortable, you can stop after a half hour, but it might be more meaningful to take a whole hour. Even if you think nothing is going on, show up again in your next scheduled time.

Pam Reitman finished her upteenth draft of her novel, and sent it off to an agent. She decided to put time in her schedule for actively doing nothing; i.e., sitting in her writing office looking at books on a shelf. She picked up one to read, and realized it had information for the character she wanted to write about next. She sat down and wrote out the outline for her next novel.

She had other choices. She could have obsessed about what the agent would think of her manuscript. She could have made lists and picked up material she'd already been working on. She could have just filled her schedule with all the zillions of important things everyone always has to do. But she didn't. She chose to give herself an open space of time to just putter, and it gave her the room she needed for her subconscious to do the work for her.

If you find it too uncomfortable to sit, here are some exercises you can try.

10 book ideas

Set your timer for 6 minutes, and then list here ten book ideas. They don't necessarily have to be books you plan to write yourself. Just write them down. Keep going after you think you can't come up with any more. In my experience, it's at this juncture that the juice is flowing and good things show up.

1.
2.
3.
4.
5.
6.
7.
8.
9.
10.

One of the points of this exercise is to show you that you have a lot of ideas. Most writers I know walk around with at least four at any given time. Another point is to stimulate you to think beyond your normal boundaries. When I do this exercise in my classes, you can feel the energy in the room shift, and everyone gets excited. Usually, when people begin sharing their thoughts, everyone gets more ideas. It may turn out that there is something on your list that you'd like to begin focusing on now. Hold these ideas lightly, and let yourself play with one or two of them in your next writing time. I suggest you explore the one that appeals to you the most, and the one that you don't like at all. Those are the ones that have the most energy.

Write to prompts

When you are not sure what you want to do next, another way to begin to access your creativity is to write to prompts. The basic idea is, you are given a topic (a subject, a sentence to complete, or an object) and a time limit, and you write on it. I have done these most often in a group setting and it's amazing how the same prompt will lead to six or seven completely different pieces. The point is not the prompt, but where it takes you. And when there is something waiting for you to write about, you will get there eventually no matter where you start out.

There are many books devoted solely to this topic. Appendix A lists several of them.

Finding Forrester trick

In the movie *Finding Forrester* (a good movie that I think is a little underrated), the reclusive writer, Forrester, begins to be a mentor to a high school student who is an aspiring writer. One of his assignments is that the student type in the first page of one of his short stories, and then continue it on his own. It is one way to get you started, and it also shows that it doesn't matter where you start, the point is to get into the flow and find your own voice. You can do this too. Take a novel or short story off your shelf (it doesn't have to be your favorite) and type the first page up. Then just keep going. Set your timer for a half hour and see what happens. Again, hold it lightly. The point here is to help you get past the critic and your fear and find your own creative juice again

Review the file of ideas you have collected.

In the process of finishing this last book, one of your assignments was to harvest the ideas that came to you, by noting them down in a file, and then returning to your writing. If you did this, turn to that file now and review it. Is there anything there that you'd like to explore? One way to find out is to take a writing session and begin writing on it. Hold it lightly, and play with it.

Pay attention to what obsesses you.

Another trick is to think about what you are obsessed by right now. What are you doing when you aren't "supposed to" be doing it? Reading obsessively about a particular topic? Staying up late to watch an old movie? Is this obsession really the beginning of an idea? There might be clues here as well to what your next project will be. One of my students used to read about history in the library at school when he was supposed to be studying another topic. It was only when he began writing that he realized that experience was the basis for the material he ended up working on. I have found myself watching what I thought was too much television, only to realize I was getting a primer on how to structure stories and use plots (one-hour dramas are good examples of this). Take yourself seriously, and recognize your own creativity instead of judging it. Take a moment to write down your obsession.

What is it that fascinates you about it?

What would you like to learn about it?

What would you like to tell someone else about it?

Is there an idea here? Spend your next writing session exploring it further.

Pay attention to what comes to you.

During the course of your everyday life, you probably have flashes of ideas. Some are not worthwhile, but some are. Honor the tidbits that come to you, treat them with respect, and harvest them. What that means is, travel with pen and paper handy (or a recording device of some sort), and jot them down when they come to you. Treat these snippets of ideas, fragments of scenes or dialogue, or topics of nonfiction, with respect. Remember the story about Billy Crystal and how he wrote two lines on a yellow legal pad that became a movie? It's about being patient and willing to harvest your creativity whenever it comes to you. Joseph Heller once told an interviewer he'd thought he was done with writing, until the first sentence to what became his next novel came to him. And Michael Ondadje, the author of *The English Patient*, said that the first thing that came to him was the image of a plane crash in the desert, and the rest of the book was built upon that.

Feed your creative self.

Read books, go to movies, museums, let yourself do what you enjoy. This is called "filling the well" in *The Artist's Way* and Julia Cameron actually uses the "artist date" or a set appointment with your inner child for fun activities, as one of the two creative tools in her book. (The other being "morning pages.")

But these are just tricks. Nothing will replace the need to just show up and see what happens. This risk-taking can feel the most dangerous of all, and it's hard to resist the temptation to fill up the space, to occupy your mind with something safe that you already know. This time, try doing it differently. Maybe once a week for an hour, be still and see what happens. Do it for a month. If nothing has shifted, try one more month.

If sitting and staring at a blank screen doesn't work, you can also try taking a regular walk in that time. (Studies show that walking integrates the right and left brain and enhances creativity.)

I hope that you will begin to see that this is the way of life of a creative person. There is an ebb and flow to the creative process, and when you have completed and let go of one, there is a time of emptiness and then you are at the beginning again, of a new project, a new baby. The only difference between this one and the first one is that now, you have solid proof when the Inner Critic attacks you, that you actually can finish a book.

Warning. I know what your critic will probably be saying:

* Well, that was just a fluke. This time you really don't know what you are doing.
* Most people have one good book and the rest are just retreads.
* You managed to fake your way through that one, but this time everyone will see through you.

It is actually my experience, and also seems to be true of other writers that I read about, that despite or sometimes because of success with the first book, the old demons are still lurking ready to pounce. It is a new project again. As I said earlier, the two most difficult things in writing are starting and finishing, and here you are again back at the start.

The antidote to this is to go back to the first chapter of this book and do the critic exercises again. Remember that the best way to silence the critic is to write again. Once you engage in the new project and begin your creative habit again, you will be able to face this voice down.

One of my students completed the first draft of her novel after a very long process of writing. She knew she had a long road ahead of her in editing it, and also wanted to make space for a new creative project. She really didn't know what to work on. The first novel seemed to demand to be written, and was based in part on real-life events so she had had a clear starting point. Now she wasn't even sure she had another book.

So she showed up in her writing time (she divided each week's writing time in half, and worked on editing in half the time, new writing in the other half). At first, a character came to her that surprised her, and she wrote about that. She continued showing up, and reading to us in class, without knowing what she was doing. She also made time for walks by herself, and deep reflective time.

And then one day, in a flash, an idea came to her. It was nothing like her first novel, nothing like the piece she'd been writing. It was a whole new arena that felt totally exciting and fun to her, and she could see a long series of books beyond the first one. She undertook the work of beginning again joyfully, and with a light heart, as she also completed her edits of the first novel.

Begin showing up as if you are still in the white heat of writing the last book. Use the same ritual you used before. And then sit. Be still. Allow what wants to emerge to come to you. Don't reflexively find something to occupy your mind. Go deeper. What is in you waiting to be expressed? If you feel a deep desire to browse some books, or doodle, or even go for a walk, these are all okay. These activities are not of the mind, and stimulate a deeper creative place.

If you are a non-fiction writer, you may feel like you aren't a "real" writer, and that if you don't immediately have a new idea, you were just one of those one-book people. Try this anyway. Allow yourself to explore what it is that you've been thinking about. *Good to Great* author Jim Collins suggests waiting to find out what the next question is.

I hope you can see now that writing is a way of life, the creative process is continuous, and the ebb and flow are a part of that. So reward yourself for your successes, your completion points, and then go back again and begin the cycle anew. This is what a writer does.

Commitment:

Can you continue to show up?

Can you divide your time?

Can you commit to feeding the well?

Has it become a habit for you now?

Conclusion

In Chapter 6, I talked about the fear many writers have of not being part of the group anymore if they succeed at completing their book. I told you if you did, you'd be part of a *new* group–the group of writers who have completed their books. Remember, in my definition, this makes you a writer (because you've been writing).

I'll never forget once, long ago, attending a book reading where there were perhaps 100 people in attendance. The speaker asked, before she began, how many were also novelists. Almost all raised their hands. Then she asked, how many of you have completed your novel? Only about five kept their hands up. It was a profound moment for me. It is not easy to do this. And *completing*, whatever your next step, is the achievement.

One thing I do know. Truly creative people, I have found, are universally generous. Having succeeded in beating back their own inner critic, they know exactly what it takes, the same way a marathon runner knows how much is involved in finishing the race.

I often think about the writing lineage—all the writers who've come before, many of whom, though long dead, seem to live and breathe whenever you read their works anew. They have been my greatest teachers. Their generosity was in leaving us these treasures. And now, you are among them.

Appendix A 

Recommended Reading

General Creativity Books

The Artist's Way by Julia Cameron, Jeremy Tarcher/Putnam, 1992

This is the seminal work on accessing your creativity. You'll see a lot of similarity in our approaches. Some of my students don't want to divert their writing energy into the morning pages she recommends, but many of these exercises are helpful.

Embracing Your Inner Critic: Turning Self-Criticism into a Creative Asset by Hal Stone & Sidra Stone, Harper San Francisco, 1993.

Hal and Sidra Stone's work is the basis for the Inner Critic work I do with students. If you want to do further work on healing your critic, this is the place to start.

The Seven Basic Plots: Why We Tell Stories by Christopher Booker, Continuum, 2004.

This is an incredible book that represents 20 years of scholarship and research. It is helpful in breaking out the basic plots for structure, but more than that, he explains why we tell stories, and what they mean to us. It's a huge book, but I treasured every word.

The War of Art: Break Through Blocks and Win Your Inner Creative Battles by Steven Pressfield, Black Irish Entertainment, 2002.

This brief book is very direct about the "war" an artist fights with "resistence," and supports artists of all types to learn the good habits that win the "war" and produce art.

General Writing Books

On Writing by Stephen King, Pocket 2001.

I've never read anything of Stephen King's but this. It's a great book. Here's someone who accesses his creativity regularly and really understands how.

Bird by Bird Some Instructions on Writing and Life by Anne Lamott, Anchor, 1995.

Lamott was once a writing teacher and this book is filled with excellent tips and ideas on the writing process.

If You Want to Write: A Book About Art, Independence and Spirit by Brenda Ueland, Graywolf Press 10th edition 1997.

This is another classic, actually written in 1938. Ueland believes anyone can write well freed from self-consciousness, anxiety and fear of failure. She recommends long walks and neglecting housekeeping. Very inspiring.

Self-Editing for Fiction Writers by Renni Browne and David King, Harper Resource, 1994.

This comes highly recommended from several students. Two editors with longtime experience in publishing give a tutorial on the basics of writing including "show don't tell," the mechanics of dialog, point of view, etc.

The Situation and the Story: The Art of Personal Narrative by Vivian Gornick, Farrar Strauss & Giroux, 2002.

The critic and essayist who taught creative writing for fifteen years gives a reading tour of some of the best memoirs while describing what makes them good.

Story by Robert McKee, Regan Books, 1997.

This is actually a book for screenwriters, but some novelists find his structure and method very helpful for plotting. He is the controversial screenwriting "guru" whom some people despise, others love.

The Weekend Novelist by Robert Joseph Ray, DTP, 1994.

This book is a program to write a novel in 52 weekends doing his assignments. Some people like his focus on scenes and plot points.

Novel Metamorphosis: Uncommon Ways to Revise, 2nd Edition by Darcy Pattison, Mims House, 2012. This is the book recommended by a student for its clever tips on revision of novels.

Books on Writing to Prompts

Writing Down the Bones by Natalie Goldberg, Shambala, 1986.

This is a classic writing book. She has great exercises, prompts, and tips for getting going with your writing.

Writing from the Senses: 59 Exercises to Ignite Creativity and Revitalize Your Writing by Laura Deutsch, Shambala, 2014. The writing prompts, exercises, and delicious writing examples in this book will inspire you to do your best writing by incorporating sensory details.

Books on How Publishing Works

The Shortest Distance Between You and a Published Book by Susan Page, Broadway Books, 1997.

This is the only book on writing a book proposal that I recommend. Her instructions and method are solid.

Write the Perfect Book Proposal by Jeff Herman and Deborah Levine Herman, Wiley, 2001.

Wait, I thought you were only recommending one book proposal book? That's true. However, this book by an agent actually includes examples of book proposals that were sold. That's the only reason to look at it.

Appendix B

Writing Support

How to Start a Writing Group That Works

Writing groups can be extremely supportive and helpful. They can also be fraught with tension, competition, and hurt feelings. It *is* possible to set up a writing group that works for you and the other members. Following these guidelines can help you avoid the common pitfalls.

First, think about what your goals are. If you want a place to get support for writing every week (or regularly) but don't need or want feedback, that is very different than a group that wants detailed critiquing of material. Some people actually just want a group where they can literally sit and write together. That works too (as long as you don't get too chatty). So here's what I recommend.

1. Be clear about what your goals are. Write them down.

2. Invite like-minded people who have the same goals. Seek to find people at about the same stage as you (just beginning, almost complete with first draft, etc.).

Writers who are further along could get impatient with beginners; beginners can feel intimidated by those on their second or third draft.

3. Get very clear on the structure and the process. Also the time limit and the person limit. That is, how many people will be in the group? How often will you meet and for how long? Is there an end in mind or do you plan to keep going for as long as the group works?

4. If you are planning on having a critiquing group, I would recommend having an initial meeting where everyone agrees to do the exercises for the Inner Critic described in Chapter 1 of this book, so that you don't have to worry about people with unhealed inner critics attacking your work.

5. Agree to a simple format, such as the following: A) five or ten minutes to settle in and say hello. B) A timed check-in for each person to comment on how they did with their writing since the last meeting C) timed reading of work D) timed feedback on work. E) commitment for writing until the next meeting

6. If you plan on sending a certain number of pages to each person to read and critique ahead of time, be sure to agree in advance on how much time each person is committing to reading. Also I highly recommend that everyone already have a first draft completed (as brand-new writing can often shrivel under the withering glare of even the gentlest critique), and that everyone have done the exercises on the Inner Critic in the first chapter of this book.

7. Build into your initial plan a time to review how the group

is working for everyone. I'd suggest after three or four meetings schedule a meeting just to discuss the format and how it is working, to get people working constructively on solutions rather than dropping out if things get sticky. It is also a good idea to keep reviewing every six months even if there are no apparent problems.

If you have a successful writing group, you can plan on taking it further, by organizing a group writing retreat where you write intensively all together.

Where to Find People for Your Writing Group

An easy place to look for people to join a writing group is a local bookstore that has classes. Attend classes or readings and look around. (Some bookstores will actually do the organizing for you.) If there is no local bookstore, try the library. Local libraries are usually happy to support writers in the community. Community colleges are another good source of like-minded people. Look first to see what classes are offered that might be appealing, or approach the English Department and ask them. As a last resort you could try a Craig's List ad or posting on Facebook or Meetup.com. You can also look for genre groups if you are writing in a particular genre. (Like Sisters in Crime.) However I think an internet-based group would have its own set of issues to deal with not described here.

How to have a writing buddy

What is a writing buddy? It's someone with whom you exchange support in continuing on with your writing. It could be as simple as a phone call once a week to check in on how your writing is going, and to make commitments for the following week, or as complex as exchanging pages as you go along, or checking in via phone or email at the start of a writing session and again at the completion of a writing session.

The same rules apply here as with a successful writing group.

1. First, think about your goals. Usually people just want some support as they go through the writing process. Think about the level of support you are looking for, and what goals you hope to accomplish. Write them down.

2. Invite a like-minded writer to participate with you. Look for someone at the same stage as you, and agree on your goals.

3. Set up a simple format for your exchanges. Be clear on the structure, the length of time for each meeting, and the length of time you will work together.

4. If you are planning to share your work, I would recommend having an initial meeting to do the exercises for the Inner Critic described in Chapter 1 of this book, so that you don't have to worry about someone with an unhealed inner critic attacking your work.

5. At your initial planning meeting, set aside time in the future to check in about how the process is working for you both—perhaps a month out. Being pro-active about reviewing the process can help forestall hurt feelings or people disappearing on each other.

About the Author

Leslie Keenan has been helping people access their creativity, find the time to do what they most love, and complete their projects for over thirty years. She works as a writing coach, teacher, editor, and workshop leader.

She lives in Marin County, California with her daughter.

You can find her at www.lesliekeenan.com, and on twitter @SFMuse.

Made in the USA
San Bernardino, CA
23 February 2020

64707253R00104